# THE JOURNEY TO ENLIGHTENMENT

## TRANSCENDING DARK NIGHTS OF THE SOUL

## JENNIFER DIEBOLD

*The Journey to Enlightenment: Transcending Dark Nights of the Soul*

Cover Design by 99Designs.com
Interior Formatting by FormattedBooks.com

ISBN 9780578518237

# DEDICATION

I dedicate this book to my maternal grandfather, who I call Papa. He and I have somewhat of the same life path spiritually. I chose to follow in his footsteps. I also dedicate this book to my two nephews who seem to follow the same spiritual footsteps that Papa and I have at least so far. The four of us are very gifted and choose the path of enlightenment.

# TABLE OF CONTENTS

Acknowledgements  i

Introduction  iii

Section 1: The Power Outside Us  1

Chapter 1: Miracles  3

Chapter 2: Physical Healings  8

Section 2: Self-Love And Healing Tools  12

Chapter 3: Meditations  14

    Part 1: Violet Flame  **14**

    Part 2: Grounding  **17**

    Part 3: Protection/Shielding Meditation  **19**

    Part 4: Cord Cutting Meditation  **22**

Chapter 4: Energy Healings  23

    Part 1: Reiki Healing  **23**

    Part 2: Sound Bowl Healing  **28**

Section 3: Dark Nights Of The Soul  34

Chaper 5: Who Am I?  47

    Part 1: Am I An Earth Angel?  **47**

    Part 2: Am I A Lightworker?  **51**

    Part 3: Am I A Starseed?  **59**

    Part 4: Am I An Empath?  **62**

Chapter 6: Questioning Our Environment  70

**Section 4: Awakening/Ascension, Remembering/Déjà Vu, And Enlightenment** 74

**Chapter 7: Awakening** 76

Part 1: What Are The Stages Of Awakening/Ascension? **76**

Part 2: Spiritual Awakening/Ascension Symptoms That Change Your Life Forever **86**

Part 3: Another's Kundalini Awakening Experience **92**

Part 4: Seven Signs You Experience If You Have A Kundalini Awakening **96**

Part 5: My Experiences With Awakening/Ascension **97**

**Chapter 8: Déjà Vu/Remembering** 99

Part 1: What Is Déjà Vu? **100**

Part 2: My Experience With Déjà Vu **103**

**Chapter 9: Enlightenment** 106

**Section 5: Universal/Angelic Messages** 110

**Chapter 10: Universal/Angelic Number Messages** 111

Part 1: What Does The Universal/Angelic Number Message 000 Mean? **112**

Part 2: What Does The Universal/Angelic Number Message 111 Mean? **112**

Part 3: What Does The Universal/Angelic Number Message 222 Mean? **113**

Part 4: What Does The Universal/Angelic Number Message 333 Mean? **114**

Part 5: What Does The Universal/Angelic Number Message 444 Mean? **114**

Part 6: What Does The Universal/Angelic Number Message 555 Mean? **115**

Part 7: What Does The Universal/Angelic Number 666 Mean? **115**

Part 8: What Does The Universal/Angelic Number 777 Mean? **116**

Part 9: What Does The Universal/Angelic Number 888 Mean? **116**

Part 10: What Does The Universal/Angelic Number 999 Mean? **117**

Part 11: What Does The Universal/Angelic Number 1010 Mean? **117**

Part 12: What Does The Universal/Angelic Number Message 1111 Mean? **120**

Part 13: What Does The Universal/Angelic Number Message 1212 Mean? **121**

Part 14: What Does The Universal/Angelic Number Message 1234 Mean? **124**

**Chapter 11: What Are The Purposes Of These Messages? 128**

**Chapter 12: How Some Of These Messages Resonated With Me 129**

Part 1: 222 **129**

Part 2: 999 **130**

Part 3: 1010 **130**

Part 4: 12:12 **131**

**Chapter 13: What Is The Next Step Of Healing? 132**

**Section 6: Self-Love And Love Of Others 134**

**Chapter 14: Twin Flames And Soulmates 135**

Part 1: What Is A Twin Flame? **135**

Part 2: What Is A Soulmate? **136**

Part 3: Personal Experiences With Possible Twin Flames And Soul Mates **137**

Part 4: Real Twin Flame Signs **141**

Part 5: The Three Classic False Twin Flame Characteristics **145**

Part 6: Coming Into Reunion With Your Twin Flame **147**

Part 7: Events Of A True Twin Flame **149**

Part 8: Ten Stages Of A True Twin Flame Journey **154**

**Chapter 15: What Is The Divine Feminine? 161**

Part 1: What Is The Divine Feminine?  **161**

Part 2: A Woman's Story Of Her Transpersonal Experiences With The Divine Feminine  **163**

**Chapter 16: Divine Masculine  169**

**Chapter 17: Divine Feminine/Divine Masculine  171**

Part 1: How The Divine Feminine And Divine Masculine Work Together **171**

Part 2: How To Awaken The Divine Feminine And The Divine Masculine **172**

**Special Message To The Reader  175**

**Reviews  177**

**About The Author  178**

**Resources  179**

# ACKNOWLEDGEMENTS

I acknowledge those who have the courage to step forward and face the Dark Nights of their Soul, so that they may choose the journey of enlightenment. This is a very courageous path to choose. It is not easy, but they face the Dark Nights of the Soul with bravery like I have.

# ACKNOWLEDGEMENTS

I acknowledge those who have the courage to step forward and face the Dark Nights of their Soul, so that they may choose the journey of enlightenment. This is a very courageous path to choose. It is not easy, but they face the Dark Nights of the Soul with bravery like I have.

# INTRODUCTION

**D**o you have the proper tools for successfully surviving Dark Nights of the Soul? Do you know what Dark Nights of the Soul is? Do you want to ascend/awaken and achieve enlightenment, but you just do not know how to? Do you know if you have ascended, also known as awakened, and achieved enlightenment, but you were not aware of it? Do you feel like you are going crazy and wondering if others out there are experiencing similar events that you are? Have you met your twin flame and soul tribe for the extra support you need?

You are not crazy. You are not alone. Many others out there are experiencing similar events you are, but they do not talk about it openly. However, more people are starting to open up about these experiences. In this book, I will touch on all these questions and more. I will show you how to survive Dark Nights of the Soul, ascend/awaken and achieve enlightenment by opening your mind to the topics, explain what they are, and provide the proper tools to survive these experiences. For example, I will expand your mind with tools such as violet flame meditations, reiki, and sound bowl healing, plus many more tips. I am going to show you how to ascend/awaken, and this book will solve your problem by guiding you through ascension/awakening to achieve enlightenment. In this book, I am going to show you where to get the support you need, and this book is going to solve your problem by opening your mind about twin flames and soul tribes.

I have numerous life experiences with everything I write about in this book. I have done a ton of research on these topics. I have found soulmates with whom I share about these experiences, and, in turn, they have openly shared with me about their experiences. Who would know better than someone who has gone through it themselves?

One can never have too many tools to survive Dark Nights of the Soul or to ascend /awaken and achieve enlightenment. What works for me may not work for you, so in this book, you will read about numerous tools. If some tools do not work, other tools will. I am sure you will find several tools that work for you. Isolation is never healthy for extended periods of time, so I will give insight on twin flames and soulmates.

I have experienced a few Dark Nights of the Soul. Grounding, which is in this book, has helped me immensely as I do soul work. Another tool that has helped me immensely is universal/angelic number messages, such as 555. During my darkest time, and believe me, they were dark, universal/angelic messages have kept me at least in survival mode, if not better. Sometimes they were the only tool to get me by until I started existing again. You will read about all these universal/angelic number messages which are synchronicities in this book. This book covers many topics that I know will fascinate you as much as they fascinate me. I am going to empower you to empower yourself. All I ask is that you read with an open mind. See what resonates with you. Filter out the rest. Always follow your intuition. If you think you are experiencing an event, then trust me you are.

I will guide you to empower yourself, survive Dark Nights of the Soul, awaken/ascend, experience déjà vu and know what is happening, and meet your twin flame and soulmates.

Love heals all. Twin flames are meant to be fun and loving and like no other relationship before. Have you found him or her, and you just do not know it? Maybe you do want to improve the relationship. Maybe you have not met yet, but you are preparing for it subconsciously. You will also read about the divine feminine and divine masculine. Do you believe in miracles? I know I do especially after seeing and experiencing many myself. You will read about miracles of all kinds. If you were not a believer in miracles before, I bet I can open your mind to miracles. Life itself is a miracle.

Who are you? I am sure you have asked yourself many times. You will read about this in Dark Nights of the Soul. That is one of the major reasons we experience Dark Nights of the Soul. It is a dark time, but the soul work is so worth it that when you see more of the light, you will be glad you experienced Dark Nights of the Soul.

If you wait to read my book, you will miss out on answers to your questions. You will miss out on wondering what you are experiencing. I know for me I was wondering what was happening to me, and I needed to research to know I am not alone and to find out what exactly is going on. This book will change your life around. This book will forever change your life. Do not be the person who lives a mundane life. Take your life to the next levels. Do not be the person who secretly wonders what is happening, but who never takes the time to find out. Be the person who wants better in life. Read this book now and change your life around. Be the person you always wanted to be. What do you have to lose? Absolutely nothing. Take charge of your life today.

If any of these topics interest you like they interest me, read and find out more. Ever want to find your calling? You can by read the book. Do not feel alone anymore. Do not waste your life away. Start reading this book today.

# SECTION 1: THE POWER OUTSIDE YOU

In this book, I am going to show you how to get through Dark Nights of the Soul. I am going to show you how to heal. My way of healing is empowering others to empower themselves. First, I will show you the power outside of us that heals you. One way that keeps us going is to see miracles so you know there is a power outside of you that can guide you through the Dark Nights of the Soul by staying hopeful, never hopeless by knowing miracles exist. Miracles are hard to put into words. I have seen numerous miracles in my life. I wrote about numerous miracles I have seen myself. Life itself is a miracle. You will see miracles in life. Those who seek, find. We live in the spiritual world even though we experience the physical world. God works in mysterious ways. God will never give you more than you can handle. This is a spiritual book. My religion is love. All my beliefs may not resonate with you, but you may have some spiritual beliefs that do work for you. I ask you to keep an open mind. Keep what works for you. Discard the rest. Life teaches us lessons if you seek the lesson in everything you experience. Lessons are blessings. Attitude is everything. Keeping a positive attitude can carry you most of the way. We also do our part with actions. It is easier to be aware of something. Knowing it is half the battle. Our actions are the other half of the battle. Face your fears. Do not run from fears. Nothing is accomplished that way.

# CHAPTER 1: MIRACLES

There are cases of miracles in the Bible whether you believe the Bible was inspired by God or manmade. Either way, there are great messages that we can learn from. Miracles can be remembered during the hard times in your life. When I went through Dark Nights of the Soul, which I will write about in section three, remembering the miracles I have seen carried me through the dark times. I kept remembering that this too shall pass. Each religion has great messages. Hold onto your personal beliefs during the hard times.

One of the favorite miracles in my life is when I was baptized. I was baptized as a kid, but I wanted to do it as an adult, so the decision would be mine. I was baptized twice as an adult. I got baptized at a Christian church, and I was immersed under water. When I stood up I felt completely different. I was also baptized by one of my closest friends who is a preacher. Then I felt totally different afterward. This was a Baptist baptism.

Another time when I was young, I had a real visit from Jesus through a dream. Jesus and I were on the deck of the house I grew up in and was living in at the time. Jesus was holding me as a baby. He let me know how precious I am, and he promised me he would be back for me.

Today as I slowly start to come out of the Dark Nights of the Soul, I can sense and know that he is keeping that promise to me. I will write more about the Dark Nights of the Soul later in section three. I know Jesus came to visit because God will never give one more than he or she can handle. One of my favorite relatives said this a lot. I do not push my beliefs on other people. Personally, I believe in Christ consciousness. Jesus died on the cross for who he is. He is authentic like me. I believe we are all Gods and Goddesses as in divine masculine and the divine feminine. I will write more about divine feminine and divine masculine later in section six of this book. We all have different beliefs because we create our own reality. Nobody is wrong or right. Every soul has his or her own beliefs. What is true for one may not be true for another. If my beliefs are not the same as yours then I just ask that you keep an open mind. Stick to what resonates with you. Discard the rest.

Somewhat recently I was looking out the window, and I saw the most amazing light break through the clouds. I was in awe of the light and the heavens. I could not look away, and I did not want to look away. The true light is a miracle. Life is a miracle. We are all miracles. Those who seek shall find.

This reminds me of another time when I was in a car in a parking lot and parked. I saw the true light break through the clouds. Then the heavens parted.

When I was a child, I planned my life as an adult. I am highly gifted, and this is a great way to utilize my gifts. Cocreation is another word for manifesting. I manifested for around this time in my life. I am now forty years old. I spoke with my inner child and manifested my own place, a decent car, and a male tabby who is an outdoor cat. Tabbies are the striped cats. I also specified that I wanted him to come into my life when he is a kitten so he can grow up with me. I currently have my own apartment, so I have my own place. I have a decent car to get me around. I also live with the kitten I described in detail. He is exactly what I was looking for. He came into my life from out of nowhere. I did not go looking for him. One day my significant other, at the time, told me he lives with a kitten who stays outdoors but needs a good home to give him warmth and good companionship. I did not even know about the kitten until that phone call. I took him into our apartment, and he is my best friend besides myself. We have lived together for two years. He came into our apartment a day before one of the coldest winter days two years ago. Schools in the area were even closed. He may not have survived had I not brought him into my apartment because the lady where he lived would not let him indoors. He is a cat now because he is three years old and growing out of the kitten stage. I named him Rockstar because he is my rock and my foundation that keeps me going. He is my star. He is of the Universe. I have another experience to share about Rockstar that is considered a miracle, but I wrote it in section six because the experience is more about Rockstar being my soulmate. Manifesting is a miracle if it is utilized for good, not evil.

When we have a desire within ourselves, it is placed there for an important reason. We are co-creating with light in ourselves. The fact is the body carries codes within the soul. Time is an illusion on a physical level. As one timeline shifts, they all shift. What we already know, and what people already talk about is also important.

So, how do we co-create with the Divine? The first step is we have the urge to want something. It can be a human urge, or it can be a spiritual urge. The second step is to write it down. Write about what your life will look like with it. Write about how it will help you feel when you have it. The third step is to act like whatever it is, is already in your life. Act as if it has already happened. Embodying it in this way is key. Sometimes memories will block you from feeling it. Let those go as we are limitless. The only limits we have are those we place on ourselves. If something is blocking it, work through that block. I like journaling or talking to myself or someone else to work through it. If you talk to someone, be sure it is someone you trust. I highly recommend being careful of who you tell your deepest desires to that you want to co-create with the light because not everybody in this world has our best interests in mind.

Our physical body wants to merge with the energy of the light and the energy of what we want, so be sure to engage the physical body when co-creating as well. We usually do not engage the body in that way. Grounding will cause manifesting to happen more rapidly and fluidly.

After the movement, close your eyes and feel the energy. Let the energy from the lower body expand into our energy fields to make it happen. Now you have the idea on how to manifest or co-create so utilize this method for good, not evil, and start manifesting today.

# CHAPTER 2: PHYSICAL HEALINGS

P hysical healings are also miracles. A power outside of you, as well as the inner Divine part within you all, causes physical healings. A power outside of us can not heal with the inner spark within us as well as when there is that teamwork. I have experienced numerous physical healings. I will write about several of them. Maybe you have been through physical healing as well. If I can get through hard times, so can you. I am merely a work in progress. Confidence and a positive attitude are key. A positive attitude heals you much faster than a pessimistic attitude. There are numerous physical healings in the Bible just like there are with any other kind of miracle. I am an expert at healing physically as I am miraculously free of most physical illnesses after going through countless struggles. I am blessed to still be alive.

Within the last five years, I was in my car. I was daydreaming as I crashed into the car in front of me. The car was stopped at a red light, and I did not see the car. The impact was so forceful that I was so close to flying through the windshield. I saw orbs of angels who I intuitively knew were Archangel Michael, Archangel Raphael, and Archangel Gabriela because these three are the three angels I have always been closest to. Time started going extremely slow as more angels entered my vehicle. The angels were there to save my life. I ended up being pulled back into my seat with the assistance of the seat belt and airbag. The windshield broke and pieces of glass started flying everywhere from the impact of the car crash. My life was spared. The other miracles are that I did not end up not getting cut by the glass or having any bruises. Life is a miracle. This was one of my turning points to get my life back together and follow my purpose in life, which is to write this book with the messages and healing to empower others to empower themselves to heal and be leaders in this world because of the paradigm shift.

I had work done on my teeth and jaw. The work went badly. My cheek swelled up like a hamster. I was in severe pain. My jaw infection was ruthless. One night while lying in bed I asked God to relieve me of the pain or to take me home as in the heavens. I went to the oral surgeon who sent me immediately to the hospital. A hospital staff member saw me right away. He had a head nurse see me. The head nurse told me I was needing to be rushed upstairs as an inpatient because I am very close to ending up in a wheelchair for life that is if I survive death. I had tests done, and the staff was able to get the swelling to go away after being there for five days or so. Before I was discharged by the staff, they inserted a tube in my arm to receive medicine on an outpatient basis. My eyes grew large in fear, and my jaw tensed up. I had to go to the hospital daily to receive medications into the tube that was in me. I was to go for eight weeks. After two to three weeks I started miraculously feeling better. I was told I am blessed because this is becoming a speedy recovery. One nurse told me she had never seen or heard about anyone, except me, healing so quickly. After about four weeks of tests were done on me to see how my health was. One of the sweetest nurses I have ever met let me see the paperwork and told me I am healed. I was asked by another nurse to continue to come for a bit still just to be sure, so I did. Finally, the day came when I was able to have the tube in my arm taken out, and it was official that I healed.

I had been a heavy smoker, and I previously smoked two packs a day. I was diagnosed after several times of seeing the nurse with bronchitis that I am young, but that I developed C.O.P.D. The initials stand cardiovascular obstructive pulmonary disease. C.O.P.D. is the stage before emphysema. I eventually cut down on smoking. I currently smoke no more than five cigarettes a day, so I cut way back on the number of cigarettes I smoke every day. The last few times I went to a doctor I found out that I am healed from C.O.P.D., and in fact, there are no traces of C.O.P.D. anymore. I have heard of people getting C.O.P.D. long after they quit smoking.

Recently I was very dizzy. I passed out in the bathroom. I was falling fast into the bathtub after I hit my chin on the side of the bathtub. As I was falling backward into the bathtub, after trying to get up, I grabbed the shower curtain. I went unconscious and pulled the shower curtain and the shower rod down with me. My head cracked open, and blood went all over the place. I finally became alert again. I am unaware of how much time passed. My head had dried blood and scabs all over it. I am still alive and healed miraculously for the most part. There are no scars on my head anymore. The accident is as if nothing ever happened for the most part.

I will now write about one of my favorite miracles. My mother was looking for a kitten for me when I was young. I knew that he is the one by "just knowing", but I wanted to see the newspaper clipping about him. I saw the clipping. I read it. I pointed to the paper, and I shared, "This is the one." We went to see him. I found out I am allergic and could go into shock. I hid my face in his fur and lied about being allergic to him. We took him home. I accustomed myself to being around him in order to grow out of my allergies by facing my allergies and overcoming them. I was able to do so. I was no longer allergic. Unconditional love is key. Love overcomes anything.

# SECTION 2: SELF-LOVE AND HEALING TOOLS

There is a power outside of you as well as your inner Divine spark that team together to heal you. Together the two work miracles. There are also tools you can utilize for self-love and healing. These tools can work miracles also. You can never know or utilize too many tools. The more tools you have, the better. These tools can be great for the dark times like Dark Nights of the Soul, as well as better times in your life.

# CHAPTER 3: MEDITATIONS

One tool is meditation. Meditation is a practice where you use a technique, such as focusing your mind on a particular object, thought, or activity. The purpose of meditation is to achieve a mentally clear and emotionally calm state. Meditation has been practiced in numerous religions, traditions, and beliefs.

There are many types of meditations. Some of the most powerful are the meditations with the violet flame, grounding, cord cutting, and protection also known as shielding.

## PART 1: VIOLET FLAME

One type of powerful meditation involves utilizing the violet flame. According to an article by the Summit Lighthouse, the violet flame creates an act of mercy, justice, freedom, and transmutation. The violet flame is the flame of forgiveness and mercy.

According to an article by the Summer Lighthouse, there are nine steps to put the violet flame into action in your life.

1. Set aside a time each day to do the violet flame meditation by simply repeating a violet flame mantra anytime you feel tense, tired, or irritated. This meditation can make a huge difference.

2. Begin to utilize the violet flame with a prayer. Before you pray, ask the Ascended Masters, angels, and elementals to come and help you. The elementals are the nature spirits of fire, air, water, and earth, and they are responsible for taking care of our planet.

3. Invoke protection before you start using the violet flame. Pray to Archangel Michael.

4. Begin your violet flame decree with a preamble. The preamble is an invitation. In the Summit Lighthouse article, there is an example of a preamble that you can use and add to. It follows like this,

5. "In the name of the beloved mighty victorious Presence of God, I AM in me, and my very own beloved Holy Christ Self, I call to beloved Saint Germain and the angels of the seventh ray. I ask you to _____. I ask that my call is multiplied and used to assist all souls on this planet who are in need. I

thank you, and I accept it done this hour in full power, according to the will of God."

6.  Give the decree slowly at first, then up as you give more repetitions of the decree. As you increase the speed, you will find they are more effective in raising your vibration.

7.  According to Summit Lighthouse, use visualizations to assist your spiritual work. Visualization suggested by this article of the Summit Lighthouse is the violet-flame pillar. As the Summit Lighthouse says, "See yourself surrounded by a violet flame pillar about six feet in diameter and about nine feet high. It can extend from beneath your feet to well over the top of your head. See the violet flame come to life as if you were looking at a movie. The flames rise and pulsate around you. Around this violet-flame pillar, you can see your tube of light, and there is a bigger pillar of white light that protects and seals the violet flame. Keep this visualization in mind while you are decreeing and throughout the day."

8.  Use the violet flame daily. You can make a specific request for the transmutation of whatever mental, emotional, or physical problems you are working on in your life. You can work on relationships in your life.

9.  Use the violet flame to heal the records of past lives. It can take a minimum of six months of concentrated violet-flame decrees to balance the karma of one past life. This gift is from Saint Germain. You are transmuting the records of your past karma. Focus on the light in your heart. Imagine the memory being saturated with the violet flame until the form disappears. Then let go of the memory, and let a bright white sun replace it in your mind's eye.

10. Expand the scope of your invocations to include cleaning up karmic debris in your house, your neighborhood, and the planet.

## PART 2: GROUNDING

Grounding is another type of meditation. Grounding centers us within our bodies. Grounding assists us with aligning with the inner spark of Divinity within ourselves. Grounding is a concept that can help you feel more connected to the earth, both literally and metaphorically, while potentially improving your overall well-being.

Grounding is also known as earthing. This is putting the body in direct and uninterrupted contact with the earth. This means that skin needs to touch soil, sand, water, or a conductive surface that is in contact with the earth.

Connect to the earth's natural energy by walking barefoot on grass, sand, dirt, or rock. Grounding can diminish chronic pain, fatigue, and other ailments that plague so many people today.

Grounding lowers stress and promotes calmness in the body by cooling down the nervous system and stress hormones.

Go barefoot outside for at least a half hour and see what a difference it makes on your pain or stress level. Sit, stand, lay, or walk on grass, sand, dirt, or plain concrete. These are all conductive surfaces from which your body can draw the Earth's energy. Wood, carpet, asphalt, sealed or painted concrete, and vinyl will not work and will block the flow of electrons as they are not conductive surfaces. Experience for yourself the healing energy of Earth that works next time you are stressed, in pain, or not doing well.

Other ways to ground are swimming in the ocean or lakes, gardening with bare hands, laying on the Earth, hugging a living tree, leaning up against a living tree, sleeping on the Earth while camping and wearing natural leather-soled shoes instead of synthetic rubber or plastic shoes.

Grounding is a spiritual term, referring to centering your soul in your body, and in turn, connecting it with Mother Earth. When these connections are strong, it can help you feel safer and more in touch with the Earth and Mother Nature. If you experience a lot of fear and anxiety daily, it is possible that you have become ungrounded.

Another method for grounding is eating food. Root vegetables are very good for this, as well as heavier foods such as pasta and pizza. Meat is also quite grounding, for those who are not vegetarians. When you are grounded and feeling centered, you are less likely to be influenced by negative forces.

Yet another way to ground is to drink orange juice with plenty of pulp.

Drugs and alcohol unground a person, and you are more likely to be targeted by astral entities while under the influence. If you want to have a few drinks, it is better to have them with a heavy meal.

As you now know there are many ways to ground yourself, become more soul-centered, and become more connected to Mother Earth. I hope this information has been informative and useful for when you need assistance with grounding.

# PART 3: PROTECTION / SHIELDING MEDITATION

Another type of meditation is protecting/shielding. It is important to shield and protect yourself from negative energies. You can visualize a diamond coded bubble around you. You can also visualize a cloak or angel wings wrapped around you. You should visualize whatever makes you feel safe. You may even visualize an armor shield around you. You should prepare and protect yourself before you do any soul work or energy work.

If you find yourself constantly drained by others create a personal energy shield for protection. This is also important for empaths and sensitives. Focus your mind and use your senses to experience the shield.

Evelyn Lim gives steps to protect yourself with pink rose quartz and mirrors in her article, "How to Create A Personal Energy Shield for Protection". The steps she mentioned are as follows:

1. Be quiet for awhile.

2. Release any stresses or tensions you feel and relax.

3. Take in a few deep breaths.

4. Focus your mind on creating an energy shield using light from Source. Make this shield cobalt blue as it is the color for protection.

5. Set the intention first. Intention matters. An example goes like this:

   In Evelyn Lim's article noted above she states, "I set the intention for an energy shield of divine love, light, and wisdom to protect me from all interfering dissonant energies that are coming between me and Pure Source.

6. For this shield, visualize and tangibly feel surrounded by a wall of mirrors. The mirrors are around, over, and

under you. The mirrors face out. Hence, if there is negative energy that is directed towards you, it is reflected back outwards. Your personal energy shield for protection is completely sealed so that no external negative energy can enter.

7.  At the same time, make the intention to allow only love to pass through both ways.

8.  With you inside this shield, you may want to visualize yourself surrounded and embraced by the energy of pink rose quartz.

9.  See, sense, and feel the completeness of the energy shield for a few moments. Hold that in place with your intention.

10. For your future reference, make a mental note of how the shield feels. This will make it easy for you to bring it back into existence whenever you need it. You will need to repeat steps 1 -9 as the shield dissipates over time.

You can also call upon your spirit team for extra protection from all people who are toxic and negative. Archangel Michael is known for being protective. You can even call upon him.

Make creating personal energy shields as part of your getting up ritual. If you perceive that there are any gaps, cracks, or holes, just repair it with new mirrors.

The protection meditations are excellent if you need to go into a crowded space.

## PART 4: CORD CUTTING MEDITATION

Another type of meditation is cord cutting meditation. There are guided meditations on YouTube, Insight Timer, and HeadSpace. These are three greats apps to utilize for meditation. The sites have guided cord cutting meditations.

Cords are attachments in your energy body to external energies such as other people, places, situations, or beliefs.

Cord cutting is the process of detaching yourself from the negative energy of imbalance. The cord cutting meditation is not just for people who are no longer in your life or who you wish were not in your life. By practicing this meditation you are not cutting this person out of your life. You are simply cutting the energetic cord that transmits negative energy.

Cutting cords of attachments is an important skill to have. It can allow you to release the toxic aspect of a relationship while retaining the love and positivity. Cord cutting can also help you release attachments of addictions to substances, unwanted behaviors, and fear about any condition or situation.

# CHAPTER 4: ENERGY HEALINGS

A nother tool for self-love is energy healing. You will read about two types. These two types are Reiki and sound bowl healing.

## PART 1: REIKI HEALING

One type of energy healing is reiki healing. I had two readings done on me by psychics before. Both of the psychics told me I should really get involved in Reiki healing. Until recently I did not know much about Reiki healing. Recently I went to a Reiki share. Individuals and I took turns laying on tables with three or four people standing around each table. The leader gave us some insight as to how to offer Reiki healing, and then we took turns laying on tables and being involved in healing those on the table. I had never tried Reiki before this event. One lady was on the table and shared one area that had blockages was her shoulder. I piped up and shared I will work with her shoulder. The healing started, and I applied what I had learned about healing from the leader. I laid my hands on her shoulder, and I could somewhat feel the blockage. I worked with her shoulder. After eight minutes the timer dinged. She expressed that her shoulder did not hurt anymore, and the blockage felt like it was gone. I am ecstatic that with the little bit of knowledge the leader shared I could naturally heal her my first time ever doing Reiki. Those two psychics may be right. I maybe should go into reiki at some point. I may want to learn more about Reiki healing and become a Reiki healer.

What is reiki healing? Reiki healing involves energy work. Reiki healing is very beneficial to have done during the Dark Nights of the Soul, which you will read about in section three. Reiki healing is about sending the dense, dark energy from blockages into the light for love and light healing or back to the person that the negative energies came from.

Reiki is innate within all of us. When we hurt, we hold that part of the body with our hands. When a child is hurting, you touch the part that hurts lightly and kisses that spot. Our bodies are made of energy. We exist in a world of energy. We transfer and focus energy with our hands. In a nutshell, this is the essence of Reiki. Reiki is a transfer of the highest energy from one being to another. Reiki amplifies and intensifies the power of touch. It promotes balance and harmony in your soul, mind, and body. Reiki is a natural and powerful practice that anyone can learn to heal themselves. This includes anyone of any age at any time. Experience the power of touch. Tap into and empower your light force energy.

You can learn Reiki. It stands for universal life force energy. Rei is universal. Ki is chi, which is the life force energy that runs through you. There are a vibrations and frequencies in the Universe that permeates all things kind of like the force from Star Wars, which George Lucas borrowed from things like reiki. This harmonic frequency can wash away the energies that are not good for you. If you learn to attune to that energy and let that flow through you, kind of like tuning into a radio station, then it can wash away static that makes you unhappy and stressed out. Ultimately if the static is washed away, your body can heal the way it is supposed to heal because this is the way it is designed to heal. This is the essence of reiki. Gratitude is key in reiki. You must be in a positive space to offer reiki. This is a benevolent love energy.

The body is a very intelligent being, and it has everything it needs to heal. The body releases everything it needs to release. We are emotional, mental, physical, and spiritual beings. We spend so much time focusing on the physical instead of the other energy bodies. Reiki will release the body in such a way that it starts to relax blockages that may be in the body. Blockages are from an emotional trauma such as grief, loss of a loved one or a pet, loss of a job, and a breakup. Blockages are heavy energy such as fear and jealousy. The blockages just do not pass through us the way love and light do. They get stuck in our physical body. When you start to play a trauma over in your mind, you may wonder why this keeps coming up. It is because the blockage is still there. Reiki starts to relax the body in a certain way, so it starts to release these blockages of trauma.

We now know and science knows that emotional stress in the body will cause physical ailments. If you work a stressful job you may start to carry that in your bodies such as neck aches, backaches, and headaches. Things that correlate with the emotional body and physical body can be healed by Reiki.

Meditate and go within. Start to connect with the life force that is inside you. Life energy is inside us, trees, flowers, and animals. If we did not have this life force in us, we would not be here. Work with it. Grow it. Expand it.

Anybody can benefit from Reiki. Animals, kids, and even senior citizens can benefit. Those who are close to passing onto the next life get peace from Reiki.

The energy inside us created this Universe. There is different terminology people use to label this, such as God, Source, life force, Universal force, and Jesus. It is all the same. The energy is inside of us and everything.

When you connect with it, peace, healing, releasing, sleeping better at night, and being happier are some of the benefits. Our loved ones appreciate us more. You will not be attracted to situations that are not good for you anymore. You will experience a greater sense of peace. Reiki heals anxiety and depression.

How do you do Reiki? Begin by taking a deep breath in and out. Breathe in again. Then breathe out. Call to mind someone you are grateful for. Lift your hands and invite that person's essence or spirit into your hands. Reflect upon him or her. Reflect how your

hands feel with this person holding your hands. Your hands may start to tingle or warm up a bit. You can not hold anger or worry at the same time as gratitude. Envision something coming from the Universe into you. It should be something healing and good as you think about this person who has been so kind to you. The energy is entering your crown, washing down the back of your neck, through your shoulders, upper arms, forearms, and out through your hands. At this point, you should feel a strong tingling in your hands. Envision your hands being able to harmonize the things they are going to heal. Now move your hands to the sides of your face. The energy will leave your hands and go into your face knowing this calm, restorative energy can flow through you, wash through your skin, and out your feet.

Reiki two teaches three symbols. The essence of these symbols teaches three concepts. The first symbol is called the distance healing symbol. There is no past, no present, and no future. Everything is connected, even at the quantum level. There is no space between you and me or anyone. The past and future are illusions. You are not really sending. What you are doing is harmonizing intention for peace, love, and healing with all that is. You are directing it to a part of the all, which is the other person. The second symbol is the cleansing symbol. A brushing away is the cleansing symbol. Brush away what is no longer useful. Cleanse it away. The third symbol is the spiral. It stands for power. See yourself as empowering that which is already working and that which is growing and is already good.

I have a close friend who is a Reiki healer. He is one of the first people who has ever healed me with Reiki. He is exceptional at healing with reiki because he does reiki very thoroughly. Each time I have a Reiki session I feel numerous blockages removed after he is done. I start off with stagnant energy and blockages that can depress me or cause anxiety. After each session, I feel complete peace. I am happy, and my aura is shining. My face is glowing. As he finishes, I am smiling ear to ear. I feel lighter and relaxed instead of extra weight I carry on me due to negative energies.

This same friend has been in immense pain lately. His knee has gone through surgery, and he is resting for the most part. When he told me we were on the phone. We always end our conversations and visits with prayer. He prayed for me after our first phone conversation in a long time. I prayed for him, and I included reiki. This was my first time, but Source nudged me to do Reiki for him from a distance. I asked the light from God to pour through my crown chakra into my body, overfill me like a cup of love, and out of me to my friend, and I mentioned his name. He immediately expressed that he felt it already. I admire him and his gifts with reiki, so his feedback impressed me. I am honored for being natural. I am honored I was able to share healing light with him as he does for me.

## PART 2: SOUND BOWL HEALING

Another type of energy healing is sound bowl healing. What is the science behind a singing bowl? When you hit the bowl with a mallet, vibration runs through the bowl. When you run the mallet around the outside of the bowl you keep the vibrations going because the mallet is slipping and sticking to the bowl causing friction. This friction sends more vibrations through the bowl, keeping the sound going and making the bowl sing. We call this resonance. When you put more energy into the bowl, you keep the sound and bowl healing. The sound healing vibrates around the bowl, and the sound travels to our ears. We can change the note the bowl makes by changing the frequency of these vibrations.

If you add some water, then the bowl will vibrate the water, and the note will change. Water is more difficult to vibrate than air, so the vibrations are now slower. Slow vibrations give you a lower note, and faster vibrations give you a higher note.

What are the benefits of singing bowls for health and meditation? They are used for prayer, meditation, yoga, and chakra healing. They have pleasurable sounds to synchronize brain waves by doing resonance on the bowls. They are mediums used to change a person's state of consciousness. You can use the bowl for meditation in the morning, after work, and when preparing for sleep. It also increases mental and emotional clarity. It can be used to reduce tension, stress, anxiety, and even anger when needed.

How do sound bowls heal you? Each type of bowl plays a different sound and has different purposes. Each has its own sound and crystal purposes. When some people hear certain sounds, they get weak in the knees. The bowl helps us reawaken. Enter the current of the sound. If the sound is right, it means the bowl and you are already in alignment. Certain sounds work with the body. Bodies have their own signature. Certain bowls align with the chakras.

The bowl is choosing you because it is energetically aligned. The binaural pulse of certain sound bowls can help regulate the insulin system, balance the endocrine system, improve sleep, and improve memory because the brain is trying to balance that into one tone.

A Tibetan sound bowl is used for your healing journey. It can even heal Hepatitis C too. The bowls are good for anxiety, depression, stress management, pain management, sleep disorders, and space clearing. Certain sounds do all this. If the sound resonates with you, it will help with all of these things.

The Tibetan bowls are geared towards the carbon-based body system. We have had this for a millennium. We are no longer operating from a carbon-based body system. We are graduating, upgrading, and downloading into the crystalline age. The Tibetan bowls are great for trauma still but still, finish with the crystalline bowls.

Set the intentions out loud when healing or space clearing. Sound bowls activate photons and activate the light in the body. They create more space for light. Some people carry such a strong vibrational field. We all know how to heal ourselves and restore balance to ourselves. The intention and sound can change everything. It changes the dial of perception. If we want to change our family situation, play a bowl. Sound bowls can do distance healing. Do not send a sound because you think someone needs it or cannot find their own way. Instead send a sound that says, "I know you know how to do this." This is the thought and intention process.

How do you choose a singing bowl? When choosing a singing bowl, it is always a good idea to go to a place where there is a bit of a range. When looking at all the bowls, try to engage the third eye chakra. If you feel a sensation when looking at a bowl in your third eye, then pick up that bowl, and play it. Listen to the sound of the singing bowl and see if you find it soothing. After playing a sound bowl for about a minute, stop and listen to the sound, and listen to your body. See if your body is relaxed. Notice if you can only focus on the sound and nothing else. Notice the sound of the singing bowl channeling to your body. If your mind is too distracted when playing with a bowl, then you should move on to the next bowl. If you found the sound of a bowl to be very soothing, you could focus on the sound. If you can go between the layers of the sound, and think of nothing else, then this is the bowl for you.

When choosing a bowl, always think about what you will be using it for. Each sound bowl has a different purpose. For cleansing, it is best to use a bowl with a very high frequency.

We all have a normal voice range. We can go very deep when we speak. We can also raise our voice to go very high. Choose a bowl that matches the sound of your normal voice range.

If you want to choose a bowl that is good for healing, then choose a bowl that has a good vibration. Most hand beat bowls have a very good vibration. You can test vibrations by playing it and placing your hands close to the bowl. When buying a hand beaten singing bowl always ask for a mallet that has suede wrapped around the wood.

Sometimes you will be in a situation where you cannot decide between the two bowls. In that situation ask someone else to play both for you. Close your eyes and listen to the sound and see which one you like with your eyes closed.

Sometimes you want to take all the bowls home. In that situation try a base chakra bowl with a deep C note. This bowl is great for many purposes.

When choosing a bowl remember never to go for color, size, or the looks. Go for the sound that you really like. The sound is a huge deciding factor in making your decision on which bowl to buy.

How do you play a singing bowl? Firstly, you want to be aware of your posture because this is a type of meditation. Make sure your spine is straight, and your shoulders are level. This way your breath can be from your diaphragm. Hold the bowl level with your solar plexus. We want the mechanics of playing a singing bowl as easy as possible. Always look at the hand that is holding the bowl. Make sure the fingers are not wrapped around the bowl. It is a common mistake. Fingers should be extended outward to shine your energy out. Bring your elbow a couple inches away from your ribcage in order to have breathing room.

Tip the bowl towards your mallet hand. This is a cleaner angle. From the playing hand side, hold the mallet in the center of gravity. The peace sign is optional. The middle finger should be two inches from the tip of the mallet. Make sure the covered end of the mallet is wrapped snug with the web of the hand between the thumb and index finger. It is a tight grip, but light as well. Use the full arm motion. Do not use the wrist. Using the wrist is a common mistake.

Press the mallet firmly in the outside edge of the width of the bowl fluidly. Rotate it around. You can do this kind of quickly to get the sound out. As soon as you hear the female overtone nice, bright, and clear, it is the sign to slow down. Maybe you can press a little harder. Some bowls like to be pressed a little harder. Listen to the sound of the bowl. The bowl will tell you if there is an edge to the voice. Slow down and breathe. If the bowl is chattering, the bowl is communicating with you. Slow down and breathe. The bowl is your teacher. It will let you know how it likes to sound. Tap the bowl with the mallet once.

For the male tone, go ahead and touch the bowl with the mallet on the outside of the bowl. Grab the belly of the bowl. Play it clockwise. The clockwise method is utilized to bring the healing out into the Universe and all sentient beings. This is how you play a singing bowl.

I had a Tibetan singing bowl. My cat, Rockstar, was very curious and so was I when it was delivered to my apartment. They are fun to play and very healing. Sound bowls are great tools for your toolbox when going through hard times like Dark Nights Of the Soul.

# SECTION 3: DARK NIGHTS OF THE SOUL

Dark Nights of the Soul experiences are scary transitions in life, but I have offered some tools in throughout the sections to get you through these scary times in your life. Just remember you are not alone with experiencing these transitions. It helps to know what to expect during these times even though it is different in many ways on an individual basis. We all ask ourselves the same underlying questions during these times. You will question who you are and your environment. You will question your beliefs and everything you have learned from society. It is best to filter what works for you and what does not.

What are the Dark Nights of the Soul? It is a process of deep soul healing. This can be a very scary process, but it is completely normal. Always stay connected to your inner light and intuition because you will always be guided, and you will be fine. The key is to remember it is completely normal, and many others experience this process. Source and the Universe are with you even though it truly may not seem like it. We are the phoenix rising from ashes and being reborn. It is a process of very deep soul healing from past hurts and possibly traumas from this life and past lives for those who are old souls. A flood of emotions may occur due to being repressed or held back for so long. Integrating your shadow and light will cause your inner light to shine even brighter. Usher out old paradigms that control and enslave society from your life. The experiences may seem like they will never end, but then there is the light at the end of the tunnel. Healing is an ongoing process, but not to the extent of these experiences. The key is to remember these experiences are positive experiences ultimately because you come out much healthier, stronger, and authentic than ever before. You discover the truth about reality. You become more aligned with your true identity, the Universe, and Source. You start to feel you can conquer the world again. It brings much freedom. You will let go of what no longer serves your betterment. It is important to get toxic people out of your life and get toxic thoughts out of your head. We are limitless. The only limits that exist are those we place on ourselves or let others place on us. We retrain our brain. Once I relinquished the limiting beliefs I had let others place on me, I started to feel true freedom. This is when I became empowered. We can truly master self-love and assist with raising consciousness and serving to better humanity. Confidence is key. The purpose of these experiences is that the baggage holds you back, and these experiences can enable you to get rid of excess baggage. You need to go through this event, so you can begin your ascension journey.

I want to share a bit about a common fear with the Dark Nights of the Soul, so you are prepared. It was one of mine, but then I saw the amazing benefits in facing this fear. It is one of the most selfless actions one can do, despite some people's beliefs. Sometimes you need to go out on your own from family and some friends you have before you go into the Dark Nights of the Soul to discover your soul purpose in this life. It can be scary at first because you may think you have no guidance system. That is not reality though. You have the guidance system of your soul, Source, the Universe, and Mother Earth. You need to start relying on that guidance system as you co-create and engage with these new co-creative energies more. You expand into the biggest versions your soul signed on for in this life. The biggest tip is do not play it small. Fill into the bigness.

Breathe. It is ok. You are going to be ok. Just breathe. Breathe, and remind yourself of all the times in the past you felt this scared, this anxious, and this overwhelmed. Think of all the times you felt this level of pain. Remind yourself how each time you made it through. Life has thrown so much at you, and despite how difficult things have been, you have survived. Breathe and trust that you can survive this too. Trust that this struggle is part of the process. Trust that if you do not give up and keep pushing forward, no matter how hopeless things seem, you will make it.

What is my personal experience with Dark Nights of the Soul? In 2017 my awareness and life slowly started changing after my near-death car accident. I kept mostly in isolation from other people. I have a cat who lives with me, so I was not totally isolated. I was in deep meditation, journaling, and healing in other ways, such as letting my emotions I bottled up this whole life and from past lives pour out of me. I let myself feel my emotions. I researched a lot to see what resonates as well as tuned into my inner guide as soon as that part of me reawakened.

I healed a ton. It is like night and day. I am a work in progress. Healing is a life long journey and not a destination. We are always healing. I was freed from any and all limiting beliefs and actions society and others placed on me, and I had accepted as my own due to lack of further understanding. I no longer live in the old paradigm. I found out a lot about the truth of reality in life.

I discovered who I am, and I stepped into authenticity and empowerment. I strive harder each day to be more divine than the day before. I have learned to dream bigger, do bigger, and quit playing it small. We are limitless. We lose relationships of all kinds for our Highest Good. I cut off those people who were toxic and negative in my life. I connected with some of my soul family. I make room for those who fan my flames, encourage me, and support me to reach my highest potential and beyond. Would you rather stay your true authentic self and build healthy relationships with like-minded people who encourage you and support you for who you are, or lose yourself by pleasing others who do not have your best intentions in mind? I love myself so much now, and I am glad I am me. The only approval I need is that of my own. Everything happens for a reason. I healed myself from toxic and negative people by giving it over to light and love. I realize everyone has a lesson we learn from. They are messengers. As you release resentments you will find that your wishes will come true. Stick with those who increase your energy, not decrease your energy.

One thing that is very important is practicing mindfulness and focusing on living through your heart. Always follow your intuition. With God all things are possible. Source never fails. I feel everything is a blessing. I am growing immensely spiritually, emotionally, and mentally.

You may be asking what Dark Nights of the Soul is, so you know what to expect. The darkness is here to keep us from awakening. You may get very hungry for knowledge and isolate to seek information. You may get depressed slowly, but it will not stay that way. God and the Universe are with you even though it may not seem like it. The Dark Nights of the Soul give you humbleness. You learn to respect yourself, others, and the world more deeply. You start to appreciate the little things more. You are the phoenix rising from ashes and being reborn. It is a process of very deep soul healing from the past hurts and possible traumas from this life and past lives if you are an old soul. A flood of emotions may occur due to being repressed or held back for so long. Integrating your shadow and light will cause your inner light to shine even brighter. You will heal and reunite with your fragmented self. Usher out old paradigms from your life which control and enslave society. There will be a lot of purging. You will discover the truth about reality. You will become more aligned with your true identity, the Universe, and God. You will start to feel that you can conquer the world again. The Dark Nights of the Soul bring much freedom. You will let go of what no longer serves your Highest Good. You need to go through Dark Nights of the Soul, so you can begin your ascension journey. Small minds cannot comprehend critical thinkers. To be great, you need to be willing to be mocked, hated, and misunderstood. Stay strong free thinkers! Keep pushing boundaries. One of my favorite mottos is one cannot be truly lonely unless one does not enjoy one's own company.

The ego is trying to hold onto everything, including your old self. The soul gets rid of who you used to be, and then the soul becomes the awakened you. Your soul is only interested in your inner journey of self-discovery. Society and education rip off your wings. The Dark Nights of the Soul wants to sew the wings back on. My favorite poem, Rise of the Phoenix, comes to mind. It is about dying to self and being reborn. Dark Nights of the Soul is a major healing and transformation. The Dark Nights of the Soul is the hardest work you will ever endure. Jesus also endured this journey. Your awareness becomes heightened. Be your spirit self. If you believe you are a spirit and do not die, you are ninety nine percent there.

What is the purpose of Dark Nights of the Soul? One of the blessings is you will be speaking your truth about Source, soulful relationships, and how beautiful love happens to be. We discover our creative spirits, our potential, and the power of the Divine and the Universe. One of the miracles is discovering your gifts from God. It is a test about how we utilize what we get through. We can serve evil or serve the world. If you choose to serve the world, you will experience true freedom. Our souls wanted us to know meaning and purpose of our lives. The purpose for each of us first and foremost is to be ourselves. We are the creators of our lives. Our thoughts become reality. We can heal ourselves. If you want to heal your mind, reprogram it. The Universe will totally back us up if it is in our Highest Good and the highest good of others. Love heals all.

Purging and healing is part of the process of Dark Nights of the Soul. It is the shedding of limiting beliefs, which heals your mind. After the limiting beliefs have been dropped, and the shackles have been dropped, you are free to go. You have a change in priorities often. Dark Nights Of the Soul can be a boot camp on what needs healing. It shows what needs healing. It becomes obvious. Then one knows what needs to be worked on. Then there is a blank canvas. You can become someone new. Paint a picture.

What are some tips for Dark Nights of the Soul? One tip is to journal everything, including dreams because it helps get it out on paper. Your story is important and special. Let it flow.

Another tip is to let your emotions flow. This is a very emotional time. This is cleansing.

Another tip is to have intelligent conversations with yourself. It helps the healing process. This may seem different at first but having conversations with yourself is quite healing.

Yet another tip is to learn who your true friends are. They will be the ones encouraging you. They will also be the ones inspiring you to reach your highest potential and beyond.

Another tip is to learn everything about spirituality and religion. Find your truth. Your thoughts create your own reality.

Practice a lot of self-love. Meditate in stillness. Listen to your feelings because they are important. Be honest because not only is it a beautiful virtue, but you will heal and transform the most if you are honest with yourself. Look at your body, mind, and emotions. Be natural. Be you. Question being you. Answer. Ask your soul who you really are. One of the key insights to keep in mind is it is you that is going to save you. Trust yourself. Another key insight is to keep in mind that the worse things seem, the bigger your mission is going to be. Energy is the key word. Become more energetic. A key positive affirmation is I am becoming energetic. Being present is very important. Self-realization is key. It is extremely important to heal the fear of

41

dying as soon as possible. Release all that no longer serves your highest greater good like fear, doubt, and self-sabotage. Release negative emotions, thoughts, and actions in order to experience more beautiful and fulfilling experiences in life.

How do you reprogram negativity? First, reflect. Ask yourself: Why am I getting angry? Is there really anything I can do to change the situation? What can I do that will help me maintain control? Third, act upon that answer. Live through your sacred heart. Heart plus mind equals soul. Breathe mindfully. Silence your mind at times to communicate. Moving out of your comfort zone and going forth and living your own truth is a path to empowerment. This is a very courageous important thing to do. Integrate your highest truths. Live in alignment.

You may ask if it is normal to go through a few events of Dark Nights of the Soul. I do not believe there is a right or wrong way when it comes to healing. We each have our own journey.

The fears we do not face become our limits. Fear holds us back from opening all our gifts. Discovering our gifts and developing them further is one of the most beautiful things we can experience. Breathe mindfully. I transmute the energy of fear into light. It is important to know fear will constantly come into your life until you transmute it into higher light energy. I thought about why I am afraid and comforted myself by journaling and talking out loud about it. My cat is great at healing. Never underestimate the power of pet therapy. I reached out to the Divine, including Archangel Michael, Archangel Raphael, and Archangel Gabriela. Grounding by being in nature and going for a walk helps. Taking a long, relaxing bath helps. Lavender is another great tool, whether it is in the form of essential oil or a candle. There are numerous tools I wrote about in this book to assist you. Some of these may help. What works for one may not work for another, so see what helps you. The more tools we have in our toolbox, the better.

A lot say they are having trouble with worrying about evil entities and energies. This often occurs when one has had a religious background because supposedly what we are experiencing is dark and evil. My insight is that the ones who experience this are far from evil, and the evil entities and energies know this. They are using fear as a scare tactic to stop them from wanting to heal, grow, and truly experience beautiful and fulfilling experiences more than they could ever imagine. Evil uses fear and trickery. Evil is trying to trick their minds to believe they are going through something that they should not. This may happen, which hopefully it will not. It is always better to be prepared if possible.

How do you protect yourself as much as possible besides the tools I have already mentioned? Protect yourself first by grounding, using visualization, earthing, and drinking orange juice. The more pulp the better. Sage, especially white sage is very helpful at getting rid of evil. Tibetan sound bowls or other sound bowls are very helpful as well. Send the evil back to the light or to God to be healed. Then take a salt bath to cleanse any remaining negativity from your body. Sea salt is best, but you may also use epsom salt. Wash your body with the salt and water. Visualize any remaining negativity being washed away and going into the light or to God to be healed.

It is important to protect yourself on an energetic level. How do you protect yourself on an energetic level? One way is to visualize a bubble around yourself coded in diamonds, which reinforce and protect. Visualize everyone and everything you want protected in bubbles coded in diamonds. Diamonds protect from negativity.

When your light shines brighter, your vibrations raise. Raising vibrations is very important to the process. I have experienced a few Dark Nights of the Soul. God and the Universe did not have that experience for my soul to suffer. I believe they are far more loving.

Evil uses fear and trickery. Evil is trying to trick your mind to believe you are going through something that you should not go through to hinder your growth.

I am writing this book to share content on Dark Nights of the Soul to open awareness to those who have experienced this event, those who have not experienced this event or are in the process of their first or any following Dark Nights of the Soul experiences.

An evolution has been happening. It is the highest evolution with mankind on Earth ever. I am blessed because now I can do my part. If you have or will experience Dark Nights of the Soul, it must be part of the process before effective ascension may occur. I will write about ascension in further length in section four of this book. Together we can raise consciousness and assist others as well as Mother Earth.

Jesus experienced Dark Nights of the Soul. Buddha sat isolated for a very long time while going through Dark Nights of the Soul. Numerous people have also experienced Dark Nights of the Soul, but they have not talked about it openly. People are starting to discuss these events more openly than they have in the past.

How do you clear negative energy? One way is to cut ties and cords with negativity as mentioned in section two. Sage is another method. Candles work when you set intentions also.

Another great way is to journal. One method is to put the person's or people's name(s) down and write about the emotions. Let yourself feel them. Write about why you are hurting. Analyze what is behind it once the hurt or most of the hurt is out, so you can empower yourself. Realize that you do not need that negativity, toxicity, or even relationships. Grow by realizing what qualities you are looking for in current and future relationships instead. Burn the paper in a candle and sage away. Please use precaution. Also, when you are ready, look within yourself to see if a part of you attracted this person or these people. This is not always the case. There is always a lesson you connected with that person for, no matter the closeness. Analyze to discover what that lesson is. Always allow yourself to heal and grow. When you journal, burn, and sage saying something like with this flame I banish any negativity from this person, and mention the person's name. Only good can come out of this. And so it is. Say these words a few times if needed, but make sure you push the smoke away from you with a giant feather. Most importantly, make sure you have protected yourself beforehand by grounding, using crystals, drinking orange juice, visualization, or earthing. Say it and feel the action with intent. Send the negative energy back to the people, the light, or God to be healed. Take a salt bath after to cleanse any remaining negativity from your body. Sea salt is best, but you may also use epsom salt. Wash your body with the salt and water, and visualize any remaining negativity being washed away and back to them, the light, or God to be healed.

It is important to be protected on an energetic level as I mentioned in section two. One way is to visualize a bubble around you coded in diamonds, which reinforce and protect on an energetic level. Visualize everyone and everything I want protected in bubbles coded in diamonds. Diamonds protect from negativity.

# CHAPTER 5: WHO AM I?

You will ask yourself major questions when you experience the Dark Nights of the Soul. You will question who you are. You will also question your environment.

## PART 1: AM I AN EARTH ANGEL?

During the Dark Nights of the Soul, you may question if you are an Earth angel like myself. You may be an Earth angel like me. What is an Earth angel? An earth angel is a broad term for lightworkers and starseeds. An Earth angel is a soul that chose to incarnate here at this unique time in history as the planet is shifting in frequency and consciousness. Earth angels chose to bring the Divine here to express out of their physical vehicle to rub off on people, so as many people as possible could ride the ascension wave. Earth angels want to help as many people as could come by spreading their light. First, Earth angels need to find the light within themselves. That is the unique journey of Earth angels. Many, like myself, come in and express their mission and why they come here. However, they get lost in the craziness of the Earth realm and challenges. Many have chosen challenging situations because once they come out of it, they will have much more of an ability to shine and help other people. Many Earth angels are just starting to waken up as to why they came here.

Multiple timelines are merging in order to serve humanity, Earth, and all souls in the ascension, also known as awakening. Earth angels are born with a wakeup call. They are born with a time to awaken a series of happenings, events, and lessons in order to awaken your Divine truth. They retain their connections with higher angelic counterparts. You have Higher Selves and higher aspects of you who have connections with higher frequencies. Connect with your Higher Self, light self, in order to serve Earth and humanity. Earth angels bring Mother Earth and humanity into a paradigm of love, peace, cocreation, and connection. You connect with higher angelic selves through your heart, by quieting the mind, expanding consciousness, tuning into ascension columns of light, tuning into your light body, expanding, relaxing, and making the connection. If you are an Earth angel, you serve others, love others, show up with love and compassion, listen, and are present. You are multifaceted. Step into full light and gifts by sharing as a wayshower, a guide, and an Earth angel who is actively supporting Earth and humanity through your unique psychic abilities, skills, and gifts. You choose to respond with love and compassion, to be a friend, and a light committed to reawakening your inner Divine light to access your higher angelic selves, accessing your true Divine nature, and shining your light. Keep asking how I may serve. How may I more vibrantly shine? Show me, activate me, and awaken me. Listen to your intuition. Silence your mind. Expand, love, and serve.

There are several ways to know if you are an Earth angel. I list seven below.

1.  You are sensitive to everything. Empaths, lightworkers, and Earth angels are very sensitive to other people's emotions. Your physical body is sensitive to most things. You are sensitive to caffeine, drugs, and food. Most do not do well with meat and dairy. You are sensitive on all levels. You may feel unease, discontentment, and agitation. As you start to awaken, you may rid yourself of all things that start to make you unhappy. You will blossom into your energy and your sensitivity will become a gift for you.

2.  You have strong and powerful instincts. Your intuition is key because your intuition is your compass. Always trust your gut. Your intuition will guide you into your light.

3.  You feel you are an old soul. You possess a lot of earthly wisdom that would normally cause you to have had certain experiences, but that wisdom is there even though you do not know why it is there. You have a general

wisdom when it comes to common earthly type struggles. You have a wisdom about you that helps you avoid pitfalls, which other people have not learned yet. You see the broader purpose of things. You are wise beyond your years.

4. You have a certain sense of purpose, not general. You feel you need to find it. The reason you suspect and know this is because you have a weird feeling when doing a certain job that is not your purpose. The way you find your purpose is by trying several things. You will know when you find your purpose. You feel it intensely when it is not your purpose.

5. You feel very well in nature. Your energy, emotional, and physical bodies enjoy it. It feels great to get away. Nature is your sanctuary. Your consciousness and aura expands in nature. We close off from negativity. You can "be" in nature. Nature helps you feel healthier and happier.

6. You experience synchronicity. Synchronicities are messages. An example is a number. For example, 000. You can read more about these universal and angelic messages in section five. Your physical reality will illuminate your spiritual path to go down the right road. You will get signs. You will notice them. If you get

synchronicity you are an Earth angel. You have a purpose. You came here to awaken to your purpose.

7.  There is a massive, epic transformation happening on Earth. You came here to be a part. It is an upliftment of the collective conscious. It is not an easy transition. You came here to help people not get so lost. You came to light the way.

By following your own dreams, you will light the way. Others get swallowed up. The more people to light the way, the more people to ride the wave of ascension. I hope this part on Earth angels answered the questions you had on what an Earth angel is.

## PART 2: AM I A LIGHTWORKER?

During the Dark Nights of the Soul, you may question if you are a lightworker. You may be a lightworker like me. What a gift this is! There were 144,000 original lightworkers. These souls are mentioned in the Bible. Lightworkers are all about love and light. A lightworker is a special person with a psychic ability to know intuitively what other people are thinking, feeling, or need in order to heal. A lightworker is anyone who devotes their life to be a bright light in the world. Being a lightworker is about helping others and the planet, and basically being a sweet person. Some people say you need to be spiritual to be a lightworker. You do not have to have a spiritual career or even be religious at all to be a lightworker. Some of the coolest lightworkers I know are total

Agnostics. To me, spirituality is not the same as being religious. Love is my religion.

Lightworkers are beacons of light in a world full of dark. People are attracted to them because of the way light emanates from them. They glow.

There is one prediction that can be found both, in the book of Revelations and the emerald tablets forecasting something very exciting! It says that there will be an incarnation of 144,000 lightworkers who will save Earth from the forces of darkness during the end times. The most interesting part about this prediction is the realization that most of these lightworkers are now here and in the process of waking up to their divine purpose and mission on Earth. Most of them might not even know or remember who they really are! According to spiritual teachers and psychics, the cellular memories of the 144,000 were programmed, timed, and triggered to go off at this time and awaken them to their true identity, mission, and purpose for incarnating on Earth at this most crucial time in Earth's history.

What does it mean to save the world? We need saving as a species. There is something rotten deep in our collective psyche and we need to deal with it. Lightworkers are people who heal on many levels. They heal mentally, physically, emotionally, and even spiritually. They do this through their work and their energy. They must learn to control and manage it. That is why they are the ones who will save the world from the forces of darkness because they will help us heal the shadows of humanity. The number is a sacred quantity that, if reached, creates a powerful wave that cannot be stopped. It creates a wave that will wash the whole world from its negative behavior that is slowing down our true potential of love. It is like when you try to stop fire from spreading. If you extinguish a certain amount of that fire, the rest will simply extinguish by itself.

Are you one of the 144,000 lightworkers that will save the world? There are ten common traits among fellow lightworkers. All of them experienced most of these in the process of their awakening. If you experience any of these characteristics you are one of the 144,000 prophesized lightworkers that will save the world.

≈ You were always identifying with heroic characters and superheroes. You still do, even if you are an adult now.
≈ You have deep purpose that not a lot of people know about. You might not be sure yourself, but you just know you were meant for something bigger.
≈ You have an inner understanding about spiritual concepts, higher knowledge, and cosmic wisdom that feels natural to you.
≈ You love people, but you hate them at the same time, and this is so confusing to you. It is like you unconditionally love who they are at their core, but you hate all the junk that is preventing them to shine. Some of this junk includes their ego, addictions, stupid decisions, and negativity.
≈ You might have panic attacks and anxiety problems.

≈   You love animals, and you feel deeply for the harm we do to them to satisfy our own needs.

≈   You cannot stand injustice.

≈   You always try to lighten up the mood. If something is tense, you tell a joke. If someone is down, you do your best to cheer them up. If someone is asking for your help, you might go out of your own way just to help them.

≈   You tend to inspire others even if you are unaware of this.

≈   You love to merge dualities into oneness, like science and spirituality, psychology and philosophy, technology and nature.

The time for awakening is now! We have reached and entered the eleventh hour of the great change that is taking place on Earth! The time has come for the remaining lightworkers to awaken, so we can get to the prophesized number of 144,000! You need to dislodge the dream of materialism, and wake up and smell the coffee, roll up your sleeves, put on your thinking caps, and be about the task of saving this world! You have something to offer this world, and deep down you know what that is. Stop following norms and trends. Do what you know you were meant to do. If you are still not sure of what that is, just do what feels good and natural to you. Do what makes you feel alive! Do what really has meaning for you! Or simply, live through your heart. Resonate with love. That is all we really need to heal humanity!

I watched a video to research different types of lightworkers. Melanie Beckler made the video. Her website is ask.angels.com. Her video is titled "The 11 Types of Lightworkers Helping Earth Ascend". I am going to share what I learned from her video. I fit into several types of these lightworker categories. See if you fit into any of them also. If not, it is a great way to learn about lightworkers. Being a lightworker can be as simple as shining light, helping, serving, loving, and sharing positivity. Being a decent human being and uplifting the world is being a lightworker. Service is essential for lightworkers.

The first type of lightworkers are grid workers and gatekeepers. These work with grids on Gaia. This could be the human heart grid that connects the heart of all awakened humans. This could also be grids on Earth that connect sacred sites through lay lines. This could also be higher grids like crystalline grids.

The second type of lightworkers are the Divine light keepers. The core mission is to embody light and to raise the vibrational frequency despite what is happening externally. They expand beyond them to neutralize density and to uplift humanity in times of challenge in balancing.

The third type of lightworkers are transmuters. One mission is diving into negativity to transmute it and release it into the light. They return to Divine neutrality, the present, and balance. Transmuters may transmute for the collective consciousness and all humanity. They transmute past karma. A lot of transmuters are transmuting along their ancestral lines, so you may have chosen to be born into an ancestral line that has a lot of negative karma. As a transmuter, you may release this, dissolve this, and help this for the entire ancestral line to level up which in turn helps all of humanity. The violet flame of transmutation is a great tool for lightworkers in action.

The fourth type of lightworkers are healers. They serve to heal humanity, earth, animals, and all beings. Healing can take so many forms. It can be mental, emotional, physical, or spiritual. There are so many different modalities. If you are a healer as part of your purpose, listen to your internal guidance about the modalities, techniques, and ways that you can be of service through your healing gifts. Heal thyself by filling your cup, lifting your vibration, and lifting yourself up with light. Fill your cup with light so you can then heal, support, lift, love, and guide others.

The fifth type of lightworkers are seers, psychics, and clairvoyants. They have opened their third eye. Readings or services are the purpose for these lightworkers, so they can inspire, empower, and guide others. This can also be seeing in areas where healing is needed or seeing areas where trans- mutation and release is needed. Seeing beyond illusion so you can clearly know where to focus energy, where to flow light, and where light, power, and presence can make a difference. All gifts and light are accessed in the present. Open and tune into your heart.

The sixth type of lightworkers are Divine blueprint holders. All lightworkers, healers, and humans have a unique Divine blueprint that is a template for your fully awakened self. All lightworkers have this, but the Divine blueprint holders actively tune into this template. They actively tune into the codes of awakening that are unique to them. They embody them and flow them forth into maybe the crystalline grid or human heart grid through service, love, or any form. They tune into their own Divine blueprint and shine this forth. This gift includes the blueprint for the awakened Earth, as well as for the awakened humanity. They tune into those awakened templates and call it forth through embodying higher light. They visualize the desired outcomes by manifesting the Divine blueprint for all of humanity for ascension and tune into the present moment.

The seventh type of lightworkers are dreamers. They work through dreaming by transmuting through dreams and astral travelling through dreams. They go into dreamspace and recognize that through dreams you are tuning into alternate dimensions of experience. Dream time is real, so pay attention. What are the symbols in your dreams? Write your dreams down. Meditate on them. Every time you remember a dream take time to ponder it. Take something away. What could be the higher dimensional manifestation of that dream? For example, if you dream that you are going to school, the higher dimension or correlation means you are studying in your dream time and leveling up. You are taking on new skills and gifts, so you can be of more service. So much lightwork happens during your dreams. Before you go to sleep, set the intention of doing lightwork to connect with your Higher Self, and to reveal to you what you most need to know. Then pay attention because dreaming is an incredible opportunity to grow, learn, discover, and to do lightwork.

The eighth type of lightworkers are messengers. These lightworkers are receiving guidance and messages from the Divine, angels, ascended masters, from galactics, from Higher Self, and sharing these messages through a video, a blog, TV teachings, and books. Whatever the media form, messengers receive guidance from Spirit, and they pass it on to serve humanity and the awakening process.

The ninth type of lightworkers are Divine blueprint creators. They can manifest. The lightworkers who weave light for positive changes on Earth are Divine blueprint creators. This could come in the form of intending and manifesting positive timelines. They can form positive events. They may even create templates into physical reality for greater love and light. This harmonizes cocreation. They not only manifest for self-interest, but they also manifest for highest interest of all beings, Mother Earth, all souls, all animals, and all of humanity. This is manifestation of its highest form. This is not only manifesting things for personal gain. This is not only manifesting your awakening but manifesting collectively for highest interest of all. This is powerful.

The tenth type of lightworkers are ascension guides. These lightworkers are ascending themselves. They are stepping into greater levels of light and share what they learn about the ascension process and about overcoming some of the pitfalls. They tune into the blessings to help everyone who can ascend as well.

The eleventh type of lightworkers are wayshowers. They walk their walk. They show the way and embody the ascension process.

They shine light. They are living in their highest authenticity and their highest blueprint. They live awakened and inspired with the highest interest of all beings on the path. They show the way through action and through embodiment for all of humanity.

It is highly likely you will embody many of these traits. Trust your intuition and guidance. Continuously ask how you may be of service. Trust your inner guidance. Keep shining more of your light and make a positive difference in the world in whatever way possible. This is being a lightworker. Being a lightworker does not mean you have to be on camera. You do not even have to be on stage. You do not have to be a spiritual teacher. You can be an undercover lightworker if that is where you are right now and if that is where you are being called. You can live a normal life while shining brightly, loving others, being of service, creating positivity in the world by embodying light, shining light forth, and being the light. This can be immensely powerful. I hope this part on lightworkers answered the questions you had on what a lightworker is.

## PART 3: AM I A STARSEED?

During the Dark Nights Of the Soul, you may question if you are a starseed like myself. You may be a starseed like me. What is the difference between a starseed and a lightworker? Basically, lightworkers are all people working for the light while starseeds are a class of lightworkers whose primary identity prior to this incarnation was with another star or planet. Many of us are starseeds. If you are a starseed, you have come from another planet and brought special skills to Earth, as your way of serving Humanity. You are not of Earth as your real home is elsewhere, and your true families will rejoin you at some stage.

You are an old soul, wayshower, and path paver who has had many lifetimes throughout this Universe and perhaps even the Omniverse. You are one of the many who are in the forefront of the ascension process and who are having the higher frequencies of light on Earth. You answered a call that reverberated throughout this universe.

If you are a starseed you came from distant star systems, galaxies, and solar systems, and you brought with you a wealth of cosmic information which was stored within our sacred mind for future access. There were strict requirements you had to pass and solemn vows you had to make.

You agreed to come to Earth during the momentous evolutionary times and to incarnate into greatly diverse and often very difficult circumstances. You made a pledge that when the time came for you to step onto the path of ascension, you would allow us to set aside your free will so that we could take whatever measures were deemed necessary to awaken you.

There are numerous signs that you are a starseed. I will now let you know about seven of the most common signs.

1. You consider yourself spiritual, not religious. You are an old soul. You have a higher wisdom and a spiritual

connectedness. You hold back a lot because you feel most will not understand you. You have spiritual wisdom that did not come from books. You were born with the knowledge.

2. You feel like an outcast. You feel alone in your own family, with friends, and at work. You are lonely. You are smart though, so you kind of blend in. You are well-liked by people you are around. You feel different, and you know you are different. You can read people and know you are alone and different.

3. You have a strong sense of purpose and do not know what it is yet. You feel it. You are on a hunt to find it. You try different hobbies, careers, courses, and so on to find what it is. You see images and signs in your life that you have purpose. Your purpose is to come here and awaken out of the dream humanity is stuck in. You are a fully realized soul in human body.

4. You feel very restricted by the burden of your physical body. It is dense and burdensome. You want to feel light, airy, and free. You feel trapped in your body.

5. You have had spiritual, mystical, and paranormal experiences. You have had out of body experiences, sleep paralysis, night terrors, and when you wake up

sometimes you cannot move. You may have experienced entities being near you. You may have experienced sightings of aliens and UFO's. You may experience déjà vu and premonitions that have come to pass.

6.  You love animals. You feel their love. You feel more at home looking into the eyes of animals than anywhere else. You feel how they are different than typical human egos and manipulative ways. You are disgusted with how people treat animals. You feel passion and love for animals.

7.  You feel homesick. You want to find home, and you long to find your true home. You are away from your primary home. You do not need to go back. Your home is inside of you. If you go inside yourself, all you seek will emanate from inside of you and outside of you.

I hope this part answered your question on who starseeds are. If you are one hopefully you learned more about yourself. If not, you now know more about starseeds.

## PART 4: AM I AN EMPATH?

During the Dark Nights of the Soul, you may question if you are an empath like myself. You may be an empath like me. Empaths are highly gifted.

An empath is someone with the natural ability to understand the emotional, mental, or physical state of a person or animal. An empath is someone who senses, feels, and reads the energy around them. They can see through ill-intentioned people.

Being an empath has its benefits. An empath can utilize being an empath as a tool to pick up on authenticity. If you are an empath, you can know when people are real and fake. Empaths can choose friends wisely. For example, I know who is and is not good for me.

As an empath, you pick up on other's emotions so strongly. We are empaths because we feel the emotions so deeply. You are sensitive and perceptive. A sign of being an empath is feeling others' emotions.

Being an empath is when you are affected by other people's energies, and you have an innate ability to intuitively feel and perceive others. Your life is unconsciously influenced by others' desires, wishes, thoughts, and moods. Being an empath is more than being highly sensitive, and it is not just limited to emotions. If you are an empath you can perceive physical sensitivities and spiritual urges as well as just knowing the motivations and intentions of other people. You either are an empath or you are not. It is not a trait that is learned. You are always open, so to speak, to process other people's feelings and energy, which means that you really feel, and in many cases take on the emotions of others. Many empaths experience things like fatigue, environmental sensitivities, or unexplained aches and pains daily. There are all things that are more likely to be contributed to outside influences and not so much yourself at all. Essentially you are walking around in this world with the accumulated karma, emotions, and energy from others.

Empaths are often quiet achievers. They cannot handle a compliment because they are more inclined to point out another's positive attributes. They are highly expressive in all areas of emotional connection, and talk openly, and, at times quite frankly. They may have few problems talking about their feelings if someone cares to listen. This is regardless of how much they listen to others.

However, they can be the exact opposite, which is being reclusive and apparently unresponsive at the best of times. They may even appear ignorant. Some are very good at blocking out others and that is not always a bad thing, at least for the learning empath struggling with a barrage of emotions from others, as well as their own feelings.

Empaths openly feel what is outside of them more so than what is inside of them. This can cause empaths to ignore their own needs. In general, an empath tends more towards being the peacemaker. Any area filled with disharmony creates an uncomfortable feeling in an empath. If any harsh words are expressed in defending themselves, they will likely resent their lack of self-control, and they have a preference to peacefully resolve the problem quickly.

Empaths can develop an even stronger degree of understanding, so they can find peace in most situations. The downside is that empaths may bottle up emotions and build barriers sky high, so they do not let others know of their innermost thoughts and feelings. This withholding of emotional expression can be a direct result of a traumatic experience, and expressionless upbringing, or simply being told as a child, children are meant to be seen and not heard!

Without a doubt, this emotional withholding can be detrimental to one's health because the longer one's thoughts and emotions are to be released, the more power they build. The thoughts and emotions can eventually become explosive, if not crippling. The need to express oneself honestly is a form of healing and a choice open to all. To not do so can result in a breakdown of the person and result in mental and emotional instability or the creation of a physical ailment, illness, or disease.

If you are an empath, you are sensitive to TV, videos, movies, news, and broadcasts. Violence or emotional drama depicting shocking scenes of physical or emotional pain inflicted on adults, children, or animals can bring an empath easily to tears. At times, they may feel physically ill or choke back the tears. Some empaths will struggle to comprehend any such cruelty, and they may have grave difficulty in expressing themselves in the face of another's ignorance, lost-mindedness, and obvious lack of compassion. They simply cannot justify the suffering they feel and see.

Empaths may be excellent storytellers due to an endless imagination, inquisitive mind, and expanding knowledge. They may be the keepers of ancestral knowledge and family history. If not the obvious family historians, they may be often ones who listen to the stories passed down and may possess the family story. Not surprisingly, they may have started or possess a family tree.

They have a broad interest in music to suit their many expressive temperaments, and others can question how empaths can listen to one style of music and within minutes, change to something entirely different. Lyrics within a song can have adverse, powerful effects on empaths, especially if it is relevant to a recent experience.

Their creativity is often expressed through dance, acting, and bodily movements. Empaths can project an incredible amount of energy portraying and/or releasing emotion. Empaths can become lost in the music, to the point of being in a trance-like state. They become alone with the music through the expression of their physical bodies. They describe this feeling as a time when all else around them is almost nonexistent.

People of all walks of life and animals are attracted to the warmth and genuine compassion of empaths. Regardless of whether others are aware of one being empathic, people are drawn to them as a metal object is to a magnet!

Even complete strangers find it easy to talk to empaths about the most personal things, and before they know it, they have poured out their hearts and souls without intending to do so consciously.

Here are the listeners of life. They can be outgoing, bubbly, enthusiastic, and a joy to be in the presence of, as well as highly humorous at the most unusual moments. On the flip side,

# THE JOURNEY TO ENLIGHTENMENT

empaths can be weighted with mood swings that will have others around them want to jump overboard and abandon ship. The thoughts and feelings empaths receive from any and all in their life can be so overwhelming if not understood, and their moods can fluctuate with lightning speed.

Empaths are often problem solvers, thinkers, and studiers of many things. The empath can literally, likely without the knowledge of what is occurring, tap into the Universal Knowledge and be receptive to guidance in solving anything they put their head and heart into. Empaths often are vivid lucid dreamers. They can dream in detail and are inquisitive of dream content. They feel as though the dreams are linked to their physical life somehow, and not just a mumble of nonsensical, irrelevant, meaningless images. This curiosity will lead many empathic dreamers to unravel some of the mysterious dream content from an early age and connect the interpretation to its relevance in their physical life. If not, they may be led to dream interpretation through other means.

Empaths are daydreamers with difficulty keeping focused on the mundane. If life is not stimulating enough an empath will go into a detached state of mind. They will go somewhere, anywhere, in a thought that appears detached from the physical reality. This is alive and active for they really are off and away.

Empaths frequently experience déjà vu and synchronicities. These synchronicities are part of who they are. These synchronicities will become a welcomed and continually expanding occurrence. As an understanding of self grows, the synchronicities become more fluent and free flowing. The synchronicities can promote a feeling of euphoria as empaths identify with them and appreciate the connection to their empathic nature.

Empaths are most likely to have varying paranormal experiences throughout their lives. Near death experiences and out of body experiences can catapult an unaware empath into the awakening period and provide the momentum for a journey of discovery. Those who get caught up in life, in society's often dictating ways, in work and so on, can become lost in a mechanical way of living that provides very little meaning. All signs of guidance are ignored to shift out of this state of "doing". A path to being whole again becomes evident and a search for more meaning in one's life begins.

These types of experiences appear dramatic, can be life-altering indeed, and are most assuredly just as intensely memorable in years to come. They are the choice of guidance encouraging us to pursue our journey in awareness. Sometimes, some of us require that extra assistance.

For some empaths, the lack of outside understanding towards paranormal events they experience may lead to suppressing such abilities. Most of the abilities are very natural and not a coincidence. Empaths may unknowingly adapt the positive or negative attitude of others as their own. This, however, can be overcome. Empaths may need to follow interests in the paranormal and the unexplained with curiosity to explain and accept their life circumstances.

Hopefully, this part on empaths answered your question about you being an empath or not. You learned more about yourself. If you are not an empath, you learned more about empaths.

# CHAPTER 6: QUESTIONING OUR ENVIRONMENT

During the Dark Nights of the Soul, you will question your environment also. Society tends to hold people back from getting ahead. Society brainwashes us. Society does not have proper values. You will question your beliefs and your values.

Materialism exists in the third dimension. The fifth dimension and above is love and light. The fifth dimension and above is higher vibration and a higher frequency level. When you are stuck in the lower vibrations and frequency levels, you may be focused on materialism. You have been conditioned by society into thinking that what is important in life is to wear expensive clothes, drive a fancy car, and live in a big and beautiful home in a ritzy area. You are conditioned to want to be a doctor, lawyer, or any other high salary career out there. In the third dimension, you may be looked down upon if you do not have any or all of this. This is the more concept. Often you buy to satisfy what you feel is missing inside. Often you buy to fill that void. It is certainly nice to have all or some of this if you buy because you want to, but not if you feel like you need to. In the fifth dimension, the values are of light and love and who you are with light and love rather than what you own or do not own. There is certainly nothing wrong with wanting all or some of this if you do not let all or some of this define who you are as a person. If you are a doctor, lawyer, or hold any other high salary career positions there is nothing wrong with that if you are in that career to assist others, not in that career field to be money driven. The career status loses the meaning when you are money driven. You want nice things, but money does not buy love. The key is your perception and intention.

You may also question the educational system. You are not your degree if you have a degree. Education is important because learning is important. If you start to feel conceited because of your degree, then in the fifth dimension, the degree has lost its purpose. In the third dimension, the college or university is perceived to be important as far as the quality of education, but if you become conceited the college name or university name has lost its purpose. In the fifth dimension, any college or university is quality because what you learn and what your professor's teaching style is becomes more important than paying out a bunch of money to go to a top college or university. When you let the name of the college or university define you, education has lost its value. There is nothing wrong with a top name college or university. It is all in your perception, values, and intentions. Not everything you learn can be utilized in life. It is about the learning experience. Knowledge is power, not materialism and cockiness. When you become conceited, the ego is taking over, and you lose who you truly are.

Life experiences are just as important as the education one receives in the educational system. There is a lot to be said about personal experiences in life. There is a lot you can learn from personal experiences that you may not learn in the educational system. For example, what you learn with the content of this book is not taught in the educational system.

I was tested in third grade for my intellectual level and intuition level. I scored borderline for both. I found out I am a borderline genius and have borderline ESP. After the test, my mother was very happy for me because she said if I continue to excel, I could possibly go to Harvard or another well-known school, in her opinion. I knew immediately I want to be a student of life. Harvard or another well-known school would have me lose who I am. I am an old soul, so this is another way I know that is the right choice for me. I have many lives' experiences and an associate degree, so I have learned numerous things from lives and received a bit of education from the educational system. I have known since third grade I made the right choice for myself. I love my experiences and who I am from the experiences. I have gone far in life as far as who I am with frequency level. I possibly could have gone to a well-known college or university also, but I do not have regrets. This has been the path for me. I have a higher purpose in life, and I have always innately known this. I have many purposes, and one of my purposes is to empower others to empower themselves in many ways during the remembering or reawakening and ascension paradigm we are currently in. I fulfill this purpose by publishing this book and starting an online business to get the messages out and to make a difference with humanity.

Society teaches sex, drugs, and getting drunk. Television promotes all this. Sex is sacred, and you should not be careless. You should treat your body as a temple. Drugs and getting drunk are done carelessly also. Personally, I prefer to be high on life instead of being careless with drugs and liquor. All three of these activities lower your vibrations and frequency level. There are more ways to have fun than to waste your life away. Being out in nature, learning, meditating, and doing yoga are just some of the few ways to have fun in healthy ways.

I hope a lot of the content in this chapter resonated. It gives you a fresh perspective on what is important in life. Priorities are key.

# SECTION 4: AWAKENING / ASCENSION, REMEMBERING / DÉJÀ VU, AND ENLIGHTENMENT

In this next section, chapter seven will be about awakening, also known as ascension. Chapter eight will be about remembering, which is also known as déjà vu. Chapter nine will be about enlightenment.

# CHAPTER 7: AWAKENING

A wakening is also known as ascension. It is a spiritual rebirth. During awakening you may wonder if you are going crazy. Many may say you are insane, but are they accurate? No. They judge what they do not understand. You go through shadows as well as light. You are not going crazy. This is normal. Everybody who is awakening is going through the process of thinking they are crazy. It is part of the process. Your old world is collapsing. You are now entering a new world. There is a lot of confusion.

## PART 1: WHAT ARE THE STAGES OF AWAKENING / ASCENSION?

There are five stages of awakening. I will also write about signposts and pitfalls on the path of consciousness. What does it really mean to awaken? It is fair to say that awakening is a journey from limitation to freedom, from unconscious to conscious. Whether you intentionally choose this path or an unexpected experience propels you onto the path, once you start there is no turning back. It is true the journey may be quite difficult at times, but no matter how long or challenging, the extraordinary destination is worth the bumps and bruises along the way. The result is freedom from personal suffering, clarity of mind, joy, peace, and ability to live a great life. The awakened state holds everything we have always desired and so much more.

Where are you, and what comes next? There are five stages of awakening and when you understand each stage and where you are on the journey, you can recognize signposts along the way and the possible pitfalls to avoid. Keep in mind everyone's journey is different. There is no right or wrong way to wake up. It is all beautiful and perfect like artwork.

Stage one is the stage of the false self. Subtle awareness of something more begins to grow. In stage one most of us are sleeping and do not know it. We are going through the motions of life. We are generally following rules of culture and the laws of the land. We do not usually question reality or seek answers beyond what is necessary for survival and maintenance of the lifestyle. Our identities define us, and we live in the construct of religion, culture, and society. We may even play the part of victim or perpetrator. Unconscious programming runs us, and as a result, we see the world in black and white and good or bad. We express a rigid model of the world as a result of our specific programming. Since there is a great desire to fit in and be accepted, it is common to sacrifice our needs and compromise our values to seek approval and be included in our desired community be that family, religion, culture, business, and so on. Self-worth is likely conditional and attached to identity or the roles we play. Because the ego runs the show, we likely believe we are the ego with little awareness that there is a greater part of us instead. Happiness is based on externals; therefore, in order to be happy we try to control reality, other people, places, and experiences. Although we attempt to control our lives, for both happiness and security, it is more likely our emotions rule and our actions and reactions are based on our moment to moment feelings. We make no connection between our thoughts and beliefs and our experiences in reality; therefore, we have no direct ability to create our reality. Despite our unconscious nature, the first signs of awakening happen during this stage. We have a flash feeling that there is something more or an inkling of doubt that makes us uncertain about life or reality.

The second stage is the stage of questioning. The doubt experienced turns into meaningful questions. The first signs of movement from unconscious to conscious occur. In stage two, we experience a growing discomfort in our lives. There is an inkling that something is wrong or missing. We begin to question mass consciousness and the validity of rules, beliefs, and laws. Things that use to bring us comfort like religions and traditions are no longer satisfying. The place where we once found answers are no longer providing relief. We question our identity, but we still hold onto it because we must continue to prove our worth, and we do not yet know ourselves outside of our human identity. As we question the roles we play, we may feel lost or betrayed by others or life in general. We may even blame religion, family, culture, government, or the world for our problems. Maybe we blame specific people for our dysfunction. We feel powerless over our lives, not yet realizing in order to take back our power, we must take responsibility. In this stage we may move from victim to survivor, but we still blame others and feel powerless. We ask who we are, and why am I here. Even though we seek answers, we still hold onto limiting beliefs that keep us enslaved in our reality we have known. Fear keeps us back and asleep a little bit longer. We may experience confusion, overwhelm, anxiety, and depression. We keep up with our lives, but we are just secretly going through the motions. As we experience a variety of challenges designed to wake us up, it turns into pain and suffering. As our disempowering feelings show up in our relationships, we get the first glance of how our unconscious programming is running our lives, but our desire to fit in and be accepted is probably stronger than any desire for freedom. Our old programs are starting to break down. We are still seeking approval by demonstrating our worth. We begin to find happiness cannot be found in the outside world. We are still playing the game by seeking happiness in other people, places, and experiences. There can be a great deal of emotional triggers. We may even experience trauma or remember past trauma. Emotions are generally very strong, and we may be almost fragile or vulnerable. What we do not yet realize is our issues are coming to the surface to be healed and released. Even though we begin to see the world in a whole new light, we may still possess black and white thinking, and maybe more than ever. We are not ready to take responsibility for our lives, and therefore, we make little or no connection between our thoughts and our experiences. As the outside world no longer satisfies our hunger, the journey inward is about to begin.

Stage three is the stage of introspection. There is immense personal and spiritual growth and the start of conscious evolution through self-discovery. We seek answers within ourselves. We release limitations that we took on from others. We may experience both grief and relief. If we spent a lifetime in beliefs that caused suffering, we may grieve for the life we never had, and at the same time, we feel great relief as we break free from limitation. As we recognize how asleep we had been, we can clearly see most people we know are still clearly asleep. Often, we try to wake them up, but our efforts are viewed as being judgmental. Others may respond with their own judgment of us in defense. We are viewed as different, weird, and maybe even crazy. Sooner or later we decide to keep our growing awareness to ourselves. Maybe realizing it is better to be silent than to be judged. At this point we do not have a lot of hope that others will wake up. We are still focused on everything that is wrong in our lives and in the world around us, but at the same time we have resistance to letting go. The process of letting go is often the work in this stage, and as we learn to let go, we leave unsatisfying jobs, relationships, family, friendships, religions, organizations, and any disempowering ways of life. We straighten out from roles we played. We reject our past identities. There may even be a total withdrawal from society. Our former model of the world is no longer working, and we no longer see things in black and white and good or bad. There may be a growing sense that we are all connected, but at the same time we may feel disconnected from every other human being. We are faced with the dichotomy of life and existence. There is a lot of loneliness. You may feel no one understands you, and you may feel there is no one to connect with. At this point you may question about why you started this journey. You may question the purpose of waking up if you are alone and lonely. You may feel when you were asleep you were unhappy, but at least you had friends, family, and people who cared about you. Now there is no one. You consider going back. You wish you could forget everything you learned about just so you could be part of a family or group. You want normalcy just so you could fit in with others, but you also know it is too late. You cannot forget what you learned. Despite your loneliness and your desire to fit in, you would not go back or undo your path if you could. Issues of worthiness often surface in this stage because the ways we once knew are no longer working. We may still seek approval from those who are still in our lives, but it does not fulfill us anymore. We are forced to feel feelings of unworthiness on our own. Our desire to be accepted is slowly drifting away with our desire to feel free and be awake. In the quest for answers we may embark on spiritual practices such as meditation, yoga, or mindfulness. If we are not using the practice to avoid something, its purpose is likely to get us somewhere, accomplish something, or to wake us up. We may experience the first real sense of power, but if the ego claims this power, we may have challenges and difficult experiences. By now we may be able to see the connection between our thoughts and beliefs and the creation of our reality. As a result, we try to control our thoughts, but it is a difficult process because old programs are still running. We no longer look outside ourselves for happiness, but maybe we do not know how to find it within yet. Peace and freedom may also take precedence over happiness. Stage three is often the longest and most challenging stage. It is also almost important in terms of awakening. This stage is marked with the swing between resistance and letting go. There are moments of clarity, but it does not last. It is likely to have more than one experience of awakening during this stage. We may believe each one is the final awakening, only to find yourself back in reality hours, days, or weeks later. With each experience of awakening, the sense of your Higher Self grows stronger. You are unknowingly making space for this self to enter your consciousness and integrate in your life. It is common to fear losing one's self, and you may struggle to maintain a sense of self. Ultimately, towards the end of this stage, an ego death is inevitable. When the ego loses hold, there is often a realization that there is no point or purpose to life. This can be liberating like a breath of fresh air, or it can be devastating, resulting in hopelessness and despair. We no longer know how to live our lives, and nothing is ever the same. There is a foreboding sense that awakening will get you everything. At the same time, there is a sense that something inside you is waking up.

Stage four of awakening is the stage of resolution. Spiritual awakening is effortlessly experienced in everyday life. This is the stage of resolution where your true self has finally overshadowed your false self or ego self. The struggle in the first three stages is over, and you experience peace and a knowing of who you really are. You are no longer seeking answers. This is fondly known as the Eckhart Tolle stage. All your beliefs have been overhauled in the past two stages, and the beliefs you now have support harmony and balance. You have mastered the art of letting go and surrendering to a Higher Power. You also have experienced and have access to the inner power you possess without ego control. Doubt had been replaced with faith and trust. You are able to see your life in such a way that your past and present all make sense. You have forgiven everyone for everything, including yourself. Unconscious programming had been replaced with consciousness. There are no emotional or mental prisons holding you captive. You take responsibility for your entire life. You are no longer blaming anyone for anything. As you free yourself, you free anyone who has ever been affected by your judgement and expectations. You are no longer trying to prove your worth. You now know your intrinsic worth, and as a result, you experience unconditional self-love. Although you might still be alone you experience a deep and profound connection to all of life, and a sense of loneliness has most likely faded into oneness. The need and want for relationships of the old paradigm has shifted, and you no longer yearn to fit in or be normal. You allow yourself to be exactly who you are without needing approval or acceptance from anyone. You no longer have the need to change anyone or help those you love to wake up. You are pleasantly surprised that some people you know are awakening. All our relationships improve, and the new people who come into your life are better aligned with who you are. In this stage you integrate your insides and develop greater understanding for the journey you have been on. You may teach, mentor, or share but not because you feel you need to. You do this because it brings you joy, and you are guided to do so. You may have a compelling desire to support others on their journey or you may have no inclination whatsoever. If you take the role of teacher, healer, mentor, or coach, you do not take responsibility for others, but rather you empower them to empower themselves. You do not take anything personally.

Others' behavior has little or no effect on you. During stage four it is common to have some spiritual practice, such as meditation, yoga, or mindfulness, but not because you are trying to get somewhere or accomplish something as in the previous stage, but rather because it feels good to you, and it is a natural expression of your life. You may also experience increased intuition and the ability to access infinite intelligence as if you have a direct line to unlimited information. This stage is marked by living in the moment. You have made peace with the realization that there is no point or purpose to life, and as a result, it is effortless to live in the present moment. Your love for your life and all that is living overflows with gratitude and appreciation as a common state of being. The concepts of good and bad have resolved, and yet, you have full knowing that everyone and everything inside you is love. You take stock for yourself realizing that you are still you. You are free from ego control and none of your authentic parts have been lost in the journey to awakening. Your personality might be quite the same, but you are more likely easygoing or lighthearted. You may have found a livelihood that is aligned with who you are, or you have made peace with your present livelihood. There is intentional manifesting, authentic choice, and truly letting go. There is no longer thought of happiness because you do not need anything to make you happy. You have realized the secret to happiness is living in the moment, and now it is effortless. You have learned how to master your thoughts and beliefs, but surprisingly, you may not have a desire to change anything in your life. Although you likely experience a range of emotions, emotions no longer rule you, control your choices, or rule your relationships. Your Higher Self has integrated in your body and you are living your life as your real self. You are finally conscious, awake, and grateful your past asleep self has, the courage and tenacity to make this journey. It is worth it.

Stage five of awakening is the stage of conscious creation. This is the stage where there is the ability to consciously create one's life from the consciously awakened state. Many people arrive at stage four and think it is the final stage of awakening, but it is a bridge to an even greater stage of awakening. You experience and deepen all the attributes of stage four, but you also step into your person as a conscious creator. Although there is no ordained point or purpose to life, you now understand the point and purpose of life can be anything you choose. You integrate this understanding by consciously choosing the purpose of your life because that is the point. Work and play merge into one, and you experience peace and fulfillment equally. You no longer do anything out of obligation or need, but instead you are guided by inspiration and true desire. You experience a direct connection to all of life. You are inspired to create in a whole new manner. Through intuitive connection with infinite intelligence, you might develop new paradigms of community building, teaching, or leadership. You can attract relationships and form communities that support the betterment of humanity. Since you have mastered your thoughts and beliefs you can now consciously create the life you desire, and live in the moment, while also creating for the future. In pure connection with prime creator, you are a pure expression in all you do.

Whatever stage you are now experiencing, you can now get it wrong, and there are no tests to pass. Awakening is simply a natural process just like the caterpillar that awakens as the butterfly. The time we spend in each stage is not predetermined, but we can move through a stage quicker and easier when we utilize the mindfulness process of letting go. Letting go is truly the secret of awakening. As more people awaken, a threshold of awakening will be experienced. The masses will awaken in a much different paradigm than those who have awakened or are currently awakening. The stage of awakening will be less defined and maybe disappear altogether. No matter where you are on your journey to awakening, you are exactly where you need to be.

## PART 2: SPIRITUAL AWAKENING / ASCENSION SYMPTOMS THAT CHANGE YOUR LIFE FOREVER

Throughout my research on awakening I found seventeen common spiritual awakening symptoms that will change your life forever. I will write about them below. Spiritual awakenings initiate you into the realm of the soul and spirit that you have been disconnected from for so long. Since we are born into a society that currently values material growth over anything else, very few of us are familiar with the mystical ways of life. Everything down to the way we dress, work, and talk, is only really the physical external reality and nothing else. As a result, our lives become shallow. We may become successful, rich, respected, loved, or even famous, but none of these things fill the void of soullessness within us. If you have come to this book you have likely undergone, or are presently going through this unnerving, but ultimately soul saving spiritual crisis.

The first symptom is sudden waves of emotion. Accept your feelings as they come and let them go. Go directly to your heart chakra and feel the emotion. Expand it outward to all your fields and breathe deeply from the belly all the way to your upper chest. Just feel the feeling, and let it evaporate on its own. Do not direct the emotions to anyone. You are clearing out your past. If you want some help with this say out loud that you intend to release all these old issues and ask for your higher power to help you. Be grateful that your body is releasing these emotions and not holding onto them inside where they can do harm. One source suggests that depression is linked to letting go of relationships to people, work, and so on that no longer match us and our frequencies. When we feel guilty about letting go of these relationships, depression helps to medicate the pain.

The second symptom is old stuff seems to be coming up as described above, and the people with whom you need to work it out, or their clones, appear in your life. There may be completion issues, or perhaps you need to work through issues of self-worth, abundance, creativity, addictions, and so on. The resources or people you need to help you move through these issues start to appear. Do not get too involved in analyzing these issues. Examining them too much will simply cycle you back through them repeatedly to deeper levels. Get professional help if you need to and walk through it. Do not try to avoid them or disassociate yourself from them. Embrace whatever comes up and thank it for helping you move ahead. Thank your higher power for giving you the opportunity to release these old issues. Remember, you do not want the issues to stay stuck in your body.

The third symptom is changes in weight. The weight gain in the United States population is phenomenal. Other people may be losing weight. We often gain weight because many fears we have suppressed are now coming up to the surface to be healed. We react by building up a defense. We also attempt to ground ourselves or provide bulk against increasing frequencies in our bodies. Do not freak out, but just accept it as a symptom of where you are right now. You will release or gain the weight when all your fears have been integrated. Release your anxiety about this, then you might find it easier to lose or gain the weight eventually. Exercise. When eating, sit at the table with an attractive place setting. Light a candle. Enjoy how good it looks. Place your dominant hand over your heart and bless the food. Tell your body you are going to use the food to richly nourish it, but you are not going to use the food to fulfill your emotional hunger. Then pass your hand from left to right over the food and bless it. You may notice the food feels warm to your hand even if the food is cold. I like to think that the food is good for me when it feels warm and nourishing to my hand. I have also noticed that when I practice blessing the food, I do not eat as much. It is important not to let yourself off the hook when you forget to bless the food before you eat. If I have forgotten, and I have nearly finished eating, I bless the food anyway. That way I do not slip out of the habit. Another thing you can do is to stay present while eating and not touch television or read. Heartily enjoy what blessings are before you.

Another symptom is changes in eating habits. Strange cravings and odd food choices exist. Some find they are not as hungry as they used to be, or they are even hungrier. Do not deny what your body tells you it needs. If you are not sure, you might try muscle testing before you choose a food to see if it is what your body wants. Also try blessing the food as described.

Another symptom is skin eruptions. Rashes, bumps, acne, hives, and shingles are common. Anger produces outbreaks, around the mouth and chin. You may be sloughing off toxins and bringing emotions to the surface. When there is an issue to be released, and you are trying to repress it, your skin will express this issue until you process the emotions and work through your excess baggage.

Yet another symptom is impatience. You know better, but sometimes you cannot help it. You want to get on with what seems to be coming your way. Uncertainty is not comfortable. Learn to live with the uncertainty, knowing that nothing comes to you until you are ready. Impatience is really a lack of trust, especially trust in your higher power. When you focus on the present, you will experience miracles, and yes, even in traffic.

There will be changes in prayer or meditation. You may not feel the same sensations as before. You may not have the same experience of being in contact with spirit. There may be difficulty in focusing. You may be in more instant and constant communion with Spirit now, and the sensations may be altered. You will adapt to this new feeling. You are thinking and acting in partnerships with Spirit most of the time now. You may find your meditation periods shorter.

A symptom is power surges that happen quickly. You may be heated from head to toe. It is a momentary sensation, but uncomfortable. In contrast, some people have found it inexplicably cold. I have experienced both. More recently I experience waves or currents of energy rolling through me. I think of the energies as divine and let go of the fear. If I think of the energy as divine and let go of fear, I feel wonderful and enjoy the sensation. If you are an energy worker, you may have noticed the heat running through your hands has increased tremendously. This is good. If you are uncomfortable ask your higher power if it be for your best and highest good to turn down or up the temperature a bit.

Another symptom is a range of physical manifestations such as headaches, backaches, neck pains, and flu like symptoms. This is called vibrational flu. This includes digestive problems, muscle spasms, or cramps, racing heartbeat, chest pains, changes in sexual desire, numbness or pain in the limbs and involuntary vocalizations or bodily movements. Some of us have even had old conditions from childhood reappear briefly for healing. Seek medical help if you need it! If you have determined this is not a medical condition, relax in the realization of it is only temporary.

A tenth symptom is looking younger. When you clear emotional issues and release limiting beliefs and heavy baggage from the past, you are lighter. Your frequency is higher. You love yourself and life more. You begin to resemble the perfect you that you really are.

Another symptom is you may have vivid dreams. Sometimes the dreams are so real you wake up confused. You may even have lucid dreams in which you are in control. Many dreams may be mystical or carry messages for you. In some dreams, you just know that you are not dreaming, and what is happening is somehow real. You will remember which is important for you to remember. Do not force anything. Above all, stay out of fear.

Yet another symptom is events come up that completely alter your life. This includes death, divorce, change in job status, loss of home, illness, and other catastrophes. Sometimes several of them happen at once. Forces that cause you to slow down, simplify, or change can re-examine who you are and what your life means to you. Forces may happen that you cannot ignore. Forces may happen causing you to release your attachments. Forces may occur causing you to awaken your sense of love and compassion for all.

Another symptom is there is a desire to break free from restrictive patterns, life-draining jobs, consumptive lifestyles, and toxic people or situations. You feel a compelling need to "find yourself" and your life purpose now. You want to be creative and free to be who you really are. You might find yourself drawn to the arts and nature. You want to unclutter yourself from things and people that no longer serve you. Do it.

Another symptom is emotional and mental confusion. You may have a feeling that you need to get your life straightened out. It feels like a mess. At the same time, you feel chaotic and unable to focus. Put your ear to your heart, and your own discernment will flow.

The fifteenth symptom is you may feel you want to do introspection, solitude, and may have loss of interest in more extroverted activities. This stage has come as a surprise to many extroverts who formerly saw themselves as outgoing and involved. They say, "I do not know why, but I do not like to go out as much as before."

Another symptom is you may have creativity bursts, such as receiving messages, ideas, music, and other relative inspirations at an overwhelming rate. At least record the inspirations, for Spirit is speaking to you about how you might fulfill your purpose and contribute to the healing of the planet.

The seventeenth symptom is you may have a sense of something is about to happen. This can create anxiety. There is nothing to worry about. Things are happening, but anxiety only creates more problems for you. All your thoughts, both positive and negative are prayers. This is nothing to fear.

## PART 3: ANOTHER'S KUNDALINI AWAKENING EXPERIENCE

Here is an account of another person's experience during her Kundalini awakening. She was not trying to have this experience. She was not even thinking of having a Kundalini experience. She feels once you reach a certain oneness with the Universe, Kundalini awakening can occur. There are those who seek a Kundalini experience and employ techniques to make it possible like meditation. Some have a Kundalini experience early in life. Some have a Kundalini experience later in life. Some never have a Kundalini awakening. If you are trying to have a Kundalini awakening through tantric methods, it should be known that there could be possible negative effects, if you are not careful and take precaution. She was simply meditating when it occurred for her. She experienced negative effects. Kundalini can leave people with varying effects. Some people experience a week, a month, or even a year of happiness, joy, motivations, and abundant vital energy. It awakens something in the soul that brings out the best in that person. For others, Kundalini awakening can be a negative experience. People may experience fear, paranoia, anxiety, obsession, anger, and more. She believes in the end the Kundalini experience is in the highest good of us. Kundalini raises the energies of the individual overall and enhances the spiritual awakening process, but it also raises heightened awareness of the self. Many with mental illnesses are dealing with the Kundalini experience, and its aftermath. Here Kundalini experience confirmed for her that spirituality is the ultimate truth. She believes there is more to life than what we are presented with for our five senses.

She was meditating in the evening and sitting in the lotus position on the floor to get her spine as close to the floor as was possible as always. Her body was aching, especially her shoulders, so she visualized herself receiving healing energy. She continuously visualized a stream of gold and white healing energy flowing down out of the cosmos into the top of her head. She visualized it entering the chakras and all corners of her body. She did this for ten minutes when she started falling into a familiar trance. During these trances, she sees all kinds of visions. The trances tend to last a half hour to an hour. Something different occurred this time. She snapped out of trances where there seemed to be hot syrup pouring into the top of her head creating a tingling or pins and needles sensation. The heat travelled inside her head. The whole process sped up. It can only be described as an unmistakable way of being intense and powerful. The intense heat travelled through her body like a wave of fire. She was frozen and unable to move as it burned its way down through her entire body. At the same time, she felt dizzy, and her head was filled with pins and needles. It was as if her head area had shorted out. Still she was unable to move, and her head fell backwards, and the heat filled her legs. After this the heat went to the top of her head again. She was stuck in a case of constant hot flashes with a swirling static energy emanating from the waist down and inside her head though no thoughts. Inside her mind were only observations of foreign sensations of what was going on in her body. She was not afraid. She knew the experience unfolding was not of her own doing. There were undoubtedly powerful higher forces at work. This state lasted about ten minutes before she was able to drag herself out of it. She could not believe what had occurred. It took a long time to realize that it was a Kundalini experience. She felt amazed and privileged. The gratefulness was short lived. After the experience, although the experience was ultimately powerful, she felt very negative right afterwards.

As she prepared for bedtime, she felt ill like she caught the flu. The next day it was the same thing. Uncontrollable anxiety surfaced about everything out of nowhere. She could not understand why she felt this way. She felt anxiety about time pressures, events coming up, things to do, people to see, and even leaving the house. She never felt like that before. Several days passed while she continued to guess she caught a virus that was bringing her mood down. However, a virus could not account for a complete personality change.

She investigated the intense heat she experienced while she had her Kundalini experience. It was a dominant factor of her Kundalini awakening. It turned out to be a classic psychic heat that is related to Kundalini and is produced by certain meditation practices. It does not have any known triggers regardless of the temperature you are or the activity of your body.

Why the anxiety? It had always been manageable for her, and no one would ever know. Most people experience anxiety frequently. She learned to control much of it and eliminate much of it throughout the years. However, the seek and destroy energy of Kundalini had brought her anxiety to surface for her to experience and heal all on her own. She knew the Kundalini experience happened for a reason. She faced and pushed through her anxiety until she had conquered it all. It took about four weeks to almost feel right again because she faced it head on. For most people it takes a lot longer especially if they do not realize what is happening. They end up needing medical and psychiatric treatment if the problem cannot be recognized or faced at all. They are therefore misdiagnosed essentially.

There is no bad Kundalini. The intent is only good. You may experience positive emotions such as elation, happiness, and feeling energetic. The effects seem as if they are only bad on the surface because once you work through those effects, you will find you are cleansed and a more balanced person as a result.

# PART 4: SEVEN SIGNS YOU EXPERIENCE IF YOU HAVE A KUNDALINI AWAKENING

The first sign is you are waking up a lot between 3 A.M. and 5 A.M. Sometimes energy wakes you up. This is when the body is most relaxed, and energy is strongest.

The second sign is closed eye visualizations. When you see visuals, light, colors, shapes, geometric shapes, and faces you are opening the chakras and the third eye.

The third sign is you feel vibrations in the body. They do not hurt. They feel good. It can freak you out if the body spasms. The Kundalini energy is bumping up against blockage.

The fourth sign is feeling heat or feeling tingly near the base of the spine or running up your spine. You may feel hot pockets going up your spine. These are some of the sensations.

The fifth sign is unusual energy patterns. The physical body is tired all the time. You may be too tired to think, and then also full of life and energy. Sometimes you need less sleep. When the fuel is activated, the energy gives us the break we need to heal.

The sixth sign is energy healing. You may experience light activations. Energy moves around in the body. It feels like spiritual ecstasy. The body orgasms. Energy is healing us. We feel lighter. There will be an easier relationship with life.

The seventh sign is feeling what you might describe as intuitive, psychic, and empathic. There is a bringing forth of real self, who is the you that chose all of this. The ego falls away. The real you will cause you to be more present in your body. You know when people are lying. You can feel people's emotions and intentions. You may have clairvoyant tendencies.

## PART 5: MY EXPERIENCES WITH AWAKENING / ASCENSION

I was born awakened. I am very gifted with "clairs" such as clairvoyant. I saw a list of twenty on Facebook once, and I have almost all of them. My mother and father shunned my experiences, and my mother kept telling me it is in my head. I shut down into a sleep for the most part since it was shunned.

I reawakened spiritually when I was twenty years old or so. Then I shut down in a slumber again because others would express it is all in my head. They said I am insane.

Then in 2017, I had a transformational experience which is life altering. I keep growing and have been healing awakened since then. My reawakening was triggered by a near death car accident. I was going to fly through the window. Then everything started happening in very slow motion. I know angels were there. I could see them as tracers and orbs. The other sign was the slow motion. Glass was breaking everywhere and all over me. I did not have any injuries whatsoever. That is another sure sign of angels.

People say I am insane or making up experiences. Always trust your inner guide. Trust and allow.

Many people are afraid to be authentic and speak their truths. They keep these experiences to themselves. Many have been coming out about their own personal experiences too though. If experiences are for your Highest Good and the Highest Good of others, the Universe and the Divine will have your back.

I found out my mind is not playing tricks on me like I had been told. What I experience is real. At first, I was a bit scared and I calmed myself down. I reminded myself they are gifts. This is from the Universe and the Divine, so it will be ok.

We all have a divine spark within us, whether we care to admit it or not. Your soul accesses the codes and insights it stores in your body. Some of us are old souls and have ancient insights. Some of us are new souls. Either way the world, even galaxy, works together.

# CHAPTER 8: DÉJÀ VU / REMEMBERING

In this chapter I will write about déjà vu, which is also known as remembering. This is one of my favorite topics. What is déjà vu? This is a very deep topic. I will also include what it is like when I experience déjà vu. Déjà vu is a feeling of having already experienced the present situation. The term déjà vu means already seen. It is an overwhelming sense of familiarity with something that should not be familiar at all. I experience déjà vu on a regular basis.

There is no one definite reason déjà vu occurs. Scientists have been studying it, but there is no definite reason scientifically. I am going to focus on spiritual déjà vu. There are many spiritual theories about déjà vu.

# PART 1: WHAT IS DÉJÀ VU?

You may be in a certain place doing something and thinking you have been in that exact place before doing the exact same thing. It can be an odd or even creepy sensation. Billions of people experience it. You may be doing something new, but it is like you have been there before.

Déjà vu in French means already seen. This may occur from doing the exact same thing in a past life. Déjà vu is you tapping into your experiences from a previous life, or you are temporarily tapping into your shared consciousness of all the other versions of yourself in an infinite number of alternative Earths.

There are numerous theories that explain déjà vu. For a few seconds we may be sure we lived this situation previously. Sometimes we can even perceive what is going to happen next. Then just as this feeling happens, we return to our normal reality.

One theory is the parallel Universe theory. The idea that we live among millions of parallel Universes containing millions of versions of your own selves carrying out our own lives with the diversity of different possibilities has always been exciting. Believers in this theory believe that déjà vu can be explained by the unsettling feeling of living a moment before as a "crossover" with a parallel Universe. This would mean that whatever you are experiencing during the déjà vu is a parallel doing the same actions in a parallel Universe simultaneously; therefore, creating an alignment between the two Universes.

Another theory is reincarnation. The general idea of reincarnation is that we lived as someone else in a previous life before we were born into this life. There are people who seem to recall accurate personal details of their past lives. Most of us move into our current lives with no knowledge of the previous lives. This means we collect no memories from our old life. Believers of reincarnation believe we come into this life with signals that reflect states of consciousness. This means memories created on one level of consciousness cannot be retrieved in another. It is like not being able to remember something you did while you were drunk. As déjà vu occurs in an abnormal level of consciousness the theory of reincarnation would explain déjà vu as the signal from a previous life. There could be a trigger in the environment which allows the transition of consciousness to occur. Perhaps you recognize a certain sound, smell, or image from your existence and momentarily remember your previous life. This could explain why we feel we are reliving the past in the present. It all comes down to faith as there is no evidence.

Another theory is the tuning fork phenomenon. What is this phenomenon? The theory goes everything in the universe radiates frequencies and produces an aura. These frequencies are a combination of our mental, intellectual, and subtle ego bodies. Usually these frequencies are uniquely tuned for each person. Occasionally, two or more frequencies can sync up, resulting in déjà vu as the experiences and emotions of multiple people become momentarily entangled. Basically, we are feeling the emotions of others who live at the same frequency.

Another theory is there is a 'glitch' in reality. Déjà vu can seem like a minor moment in your lifetime, which you soon forget after it happens. Glitch theory is a momentary breakdown in our reality. Einstein believed time does not exist. I feel he is right. Time is a human creation made to establish order and structure. However, time might simply be an illusion from which déjà vu gives us a small break. This would explain why we feel we have lived the moment before. The past, present, and future are all happening simultaneously; therefore, when déjà vu occurs we are simply slipping into greater levels of consciousness where we live more than one experience at the same time. If déjà vu is really a 'glitch' in reality this may mean damage to the foundations of our Universe are created whenever déjà vu occurs. Some say these are the moments when UFOs can be sighted. Déjà vu opens bridges between different realities.

Another theory is parallel Universes. In quantum physics the theory of multiverses states universes can exist parallel to each other. As time evolves, universes exist on different wavelengths. Naturally, we are coherent with ours but confused with others. This is like tuning a radio, so it is in tune with one frequency at a time. Déjà vu could be the brief experience of tuning into another universe.

Another theory I will write about is precognitive dreams. Some argue that the feeling of knowing exactly what will happen next cannot only be the result of familiar memory fragments. Perhaps our dreams can tell us about what we are going to experience in the future. There are interesting similarities between dreams and future experiences. People can recall dreams eerily like experiences they were yet to perceive. Are we experiencing events in our dreams before they happen? I say we can. I have had many dreams like this.

Some describe **déjà vu** as the recollection of past lives. Cases of reincarnation involve people allegedly experiencing memories of someone from the past. People have felt bursts of past life emotions when visiting a location for the first time. People have also been able to spontaneously find past life homes and locations with great familiarity in an unfamiliar place. Perhaps the phenomenon is an indication of what was already experienced in another life.

What are your thoughts? I wrote about theories which resonate with me. Not all the theories may resonate with you. Maybe all these theories resonate with you. Maybe none of these theories resonate with you, but the theories may have opened your mind or sparked your interest.

## PART 2: MY EXPERIENCE WITH DÉJÀ VU

I get déjà vu frequently. Sometimes more frequently than other times. I love getting déjà vu because I am very spiritual, and this topic highly fascinates me. Hopefully déjà vu fascinates you as much as it fascinates me. I have had déjà vu since as early of an age as I can remember.

I went to a neurologist when I was in my early twenties to see if there was an issue with my brain misfiring. I had an at home EEG with a tape recorder in my pocket. Anytime I had a déjà vu experience I was told to touch the play button on the tape recorder, and I was to press stop when the déjà vu experience was over. This way the neurologist knew what to focus on when getting results for me.

When I received the results there was nothing to tell me. There was nothing my brain was doing differently during the déjà vu moments. There are no scientific explanations of déjà vu.

I am experiencing many spiritual moments, and some days the entire day is spiritual. I am very connected with Source and the Divine.

As I wrote about earlier, I shut down when my awakening was shunned. I still had déjà vu experiences when I was asleep, but there were fewer experiences. The experiences were very real, so nobody could convince me they were not real.

People may say you are insane or making up experiences. This does not mean do not seek medical attention if need be though. Always trust your inner guide.

If experiences are for my highest good and the highest good of others, the Universe and the Divine have my back.

I remember a dream I had when I was a kid. It was an amazing and beautiful dream. Jesus was on the deck in the back of the house. He was holding me. He told me I am precious, and he will come back for me. There is a poem called "Footprints in the

Sand". In the poem, Jesus mentions he never leaves as you may think he does during your hard times.

I always recommend doing your own research to see what resonates with you. I write about experiences and research that resonates with me, and I filter out the rest.

Your soul has insights stored in yourselves. Your soul will reveal more over time. We are souls. Your soul will remind you more, and you will remember what your soul stores on an individual path. Then we meet as a collective in this oneness. Your soul does this by accessing wisdom and insights in your body. Some of us are old souls and have ancient insights, and some of us are new souls. We all have a divine spark within us, whether we care to admit it or not.

As you read there are many theories on déjà vu. There is no hardcore evidence as to what causes these phenomena. Scientists do not have solid answers. Déjà vu is a spiritual experience. What you feel is true is true for you. Trust your inner guide. If you feel you experienced déjà vu then you probably did.

# CHAPTER 9: ENLIGHTENMENT

**W**hat is enlightenment? Enlightenment is ultimate transformation. You know now and live with freedom. The enlightenments are the stepping stones and synchronicities that guide you to awakening. The actual time it takes between each depends on the soul and its spiritual maturity.

Once you are awakened, you start to search for the truths in the world, in your life, and in yourself. This will set you on a path to enlightenment. You want to know the reason for your life. You also want to know if you can change yourself, your feelings, and your thoughts. You want to know the reason why people are so cruel and negative and do not see it themselves. Just as Jesus said: when you start to search for truths, you will find the truth.

As soon as you start to search the path to enlightenment, a path will guide you to understand yourself, life, and the world bounded to the physical plane with an ego perspective. You long to let go of the ego perspective and to embrace the higher and more positive understanding that you are not a human, but an immortal energetic positive soul.

Enlightenment is to understand the perspective of the soul, which is the construction of humans, souls, and life. Enlightenment means literally to see negative situations and negative people in a pure positive way that life becomes lighter, easier, happier, and more fun. This is also a way I heal. It is called transmuting. Many lightworkers as discussed in section three heal by transmuting. Light is pure positive energy vibrating on high frequency. Light is love, and love is light. Our souls are love and light. It is who we are as an immaterial pure positive energetic being with an esoteric light shiny body.

The reason of everyone's life is to grow above the negativity of our own egoistic grey and negative ego perspective. Another reason is to grow above the negativity of life, by formulating pure positive thoughts in good and bad situations. This is good for you, other people in the world and beyond, as well as nature.

I find the good in everybody. We are not bad people just good people with bad behaviors unless we choose otherwise. I like to find the positive in every lesson. Every lesson has a blessing.

A negative emotion is just a signal of your Higher Self that you are thinking something that is not good for you, others, and nature. Transform your thoughts consciously and subconsciously from negative to positive and you will create positive emotions and feel good. This will make your life easy, in balance, lighter, and you experience true happiness. This is the only way to create balance in yourself, balance between humans and others, and balance with nature. As an enlightened person you do not experience negative emotions anymore because you always create pure positive thoughts, like Jesus did.

At the same time your soul becomes free, can travel through the astral world, and contact other beings, spirit guides, passed over souls, lost souls, or contact oneness and copy information that is good for you from the collect and in Oneness. This is called the Akashic records. I remember being in the Akashic Library and writing what life I want. I remember wanting to remain authentic no matter what. This is still very important to me. I do not need to seek the approval of others. My opinion of myself is what matters most.

At the same time all answers will arise in your mind for all problems in the world. By formulating pure positive thoughts, you raise your frequency to the same level as your Higher Self does. You become one soul.

Awakening is to see yourself, your life, and the world in the honest and objective perspective. This awakening creates the desire for you to walk the path of enlightenment. When you reach enlightenment, you will be a pure positive energetic soul that projects itself into a pure positive human being. This is called enlightenment.

I was enlightened as a kid, but I lost myself many times. By going through the Dark Nights of the Soul, I am becoming truly happy again. I am on the path to enlightenment once again as I am already awakened. Each person's journey is different. Right now, you are right where we are meant to be for the time being.

# SECTION 5: UNIVERSAL / ANGELIC MESSAGES

# CHAPTER 10: UNIVERSAL / ANGELIC NUMBER MESSAGES

W hen I was experiencing my transformation from Dark Nights of the Soul through awakening, also known as ascension, it was too dark in my life. Some souls go through this transformation once in their lives, but many souls experience this transformation more often. The great news is that angel message numbers also known as universal message numbers were one of the motivators and inspirations that kept me going as I was barely surviving. I clung onto these messages. This carried me through these dark times. The truth is until one sees the darkness, he or she will not truly experience the true light fully as one is meant to in life. It can be a bumpy life with ups and downs, but what does not kill us causes us to be stronger. I want to express this to you, so you can utilize these messages as well.

These were mostly numbers on clocks and license plates, but the messages can be seen consecutively literally anywhere.

Each angel message, also known as a universal message, symbolizes other meanings. When we see numbers continuously pop up, the Universe is wanting to get our attention. These numbers come to us from our angels, the Universe's Creative Source, our Higher Selves and loved ones on this side, as well as on the other side.

## PART 1: WHAT DOES THE UNIVERSAL / ANGELIC NUMBER MESSAGE 000 MEAN?

000 is a message of love from our Creator, carried to us by our guardian angels. Angel number 000 is a positive sign that you are in alignment with powerful spiritual energies that can provide you with the answers you seek. These are beautiful messages. I love hearing the Creator loves me. I feel aligned with the Divine. I feel I can find the answers I seek as we co-create.

## PART 2: WHAT DOES THE UNIVERSAL / ANGELIC NUMBER MESSAGE 111 MEAN?

Another universal message, also known as an angelic message, is the number sequence 111. The number 111 is known to tell you to be very aware of your thoughts, and only think about what you want, not what you do not want. This will help those positive thoughts quickly manifest into a reality.

The number 111 is a sign that the gate of opportunity is open. The thoughts you are thinking are manifesting at record speed. It is the ideal time to make use of this manifestation. If you wait too long, you might miss your chance.

Many also claim that the number 111 is a message from your angels or your spirit guides. It is their way of telling you that the universe is open to you, and your thoughts and ideas are ready to be manifested.

The importance of positive thinking cannot be overstated when you come across a 111. It is so important to pay special attention to your thoughts to manifest your desires. You must use positive affirmations and an optimistic attitude to make the most of the number 111. This will help you achieve your goals and aspirations. This will help you see your spiritual life purpose as well as your soul mission.

If you come across this number during your life, consider yourself very fortunate. It is an angel number that encourages you to rely upon your inner wisdom and your intuition to guide you. It is a number that will help you bring out the best in yourself and make further progress down your life path.

## PART 3: WHAT DOES THE UNIVERSAL / ANGELIC NUMBER MESSAGE 222 MEAN?

222 represents balance, harmony, peace, faith, strength, hope, and joy. We are going to take the stingers out, so our bodies can

become back into balance. Once our bodies are in balance again, we have earned the lives we want and deserve. We will become the ferocious tigers. This message can also be expressing that our soulmates are on his/her way to us. This message can also even be a wake-up call when we ask if we need to ask for guidance and assistance or even delegate responsibilities.

## PART 4: WHAT DOES THE UNIVERSAL / ANGELIC NUMBER MESSAGE 333 MEAN?

333 is expressing that we are heavily supported by the Trinity of the Father, the Son, and the Holy Spirit or heavily supported by the Divine. This message lets us know we have their attention. It is time to ask ourselves if we are ready to work with them. It is now time to meditate more often, as well as to read spiritual books more often. This message is expressing something in the past is currently affecting our present times in major ways. We now will want to tune in and ask the Divine for guidance with energy in clearing this situation, so it does not affect our futures. These messages can be positive messages, and in these scenarios, we fuse with more positivity to have a more positive future. We will now want to ask for resources to make that happen.

## PART 5: WHAT DOES THE UNIVERSAL / ANGELIC NUMBER MESSAGE 444 MEAN?

444 is letting us know angels want to work with us more. There is a ton of information out there nowadays. We need to sort through

this information because there is junk, but there is also quality. It is best to follow our intuition regarding this matter. There are YouTube videos and books to name a few resources. There are books on meeting our guardian angels. The more we are in the angelic energy, the more we can work with the angels. There are also guided meditations to utilize.

## PART 6: WHAT DOES THE UNIVERSAL / ANGELIC NUMBER MESSAGE 555 MEAN?

555 expresses that change is on its way. Change is needed. These changes will happen quickly. This is the type of change that causes pure chaos, which can be good chaos. The message is a wake-up call to let us know to get grounded and peaceful now instead of waiting for the change to start. A great idea is to find a guided meditation that works for you. Another great idea is to start working with a reiki practitioner. It is best to not try to figure out what the change is going to be. Instead, we want to be prepared with grounding and peace.

## PART 7: WHAT DOES THE UNIVERSAL / ANGELIC NUMBER 666 MEAN?

666 expresses abundance, wealth, and optimism. This message is associated with the root chakra, which is the chakra that represents Earth energy. This message lets us know finances are coming to us, or this message can give us ideas on ways we can get finances. This message also may express we are ready for wild

and fun sexual lives. We do not want to suppress our urges. It is best to choose a safe partner and a safe place to embrace, own, and wildly explore these urges.

## PART 8: WHAT DOES THE UNIVERSAL / ANGELIC NUMBER 777 MEAN?

777 represents a higher vibration. This message expresses spiritual evolvement. We grow exponentially spiritually. We may feel off or blockages, so 777 is letting us know we are on track, and we are not blocked. 777 is a comfort message because 777 is letting us know not to worry. When this message comes up, it is a wake-up call to get back to our spiritual lives again if we were not currently living spiritual lives. An important question to ask ourselves is what we can do to feed our spiritual lives in fun, yet righteous ways. This message is expressing the fact that our intuition is on fire. Our auras may be shining brightly.

## PART 9: WHAT DOES THE UNIVERSAL / ANGELIC NUMBER 888 MEAN?

888 represents prosperity coming our way. This message also expresses exploring something new that we may have been wanting to try. 888 is a magician's number. There is the infinity sign above his head on tarot cards. Now is the time to blend intuition with physical tools we have. An example is opening Google Docs on our laptops and channeling as we type. Another

example is artwork. We can utilize channeling to guide us with artwork. We are in Magician's mode.

## PART 10: WHAT DOES THE UNIVERSAL / ANGELIC NUMBER 999 MEAN?

999 represents completion. Something is coming to an end, or we need to put something to an end. Examples include serious talks, changing or stopping behaviors, changing course, and changing degrees at the universities we attend.

When this message comes up, there are important questions to ask ourselves. One question is do I feel there is better. What needs to end? The message is strongly expressing that what we are thinking of or wondering about that needs to end, does need to end. We need to end it, so it is on our terms, and will end no matter what, but it will not be comfortable. We will need to end it on good terms and in the best interest for most.

## PART 11: WHAT DOES THE UNIVERSAL / ANGELIC NUMBER 1010 MEAN?

1010 is yet another universal number message known also as an angelic number message. 1010 is a newer message to me, along with 1111, 1212, and 1234. You can soon read about 1111, 1212, and 1234 after 1010. As mentioned earlier these universal/angelic number messages got me through my recent Dark Nights of the Soul, and they are great for any hard times in life, as well as great times in life. These number messages are good for any time, not just when we need strength to carry on through very dark times. We all need motivation and inspiration no matter where we are in life, right?

1010 is a sign that your angels are waiting in the wings to offer support. Angel number 1010 is a call to stay optimistic and to focus on where you are and where you are going. It is an encouragement to heighten the vibration, connect with a higher divine power, and attract abundance.

While most of us would write off angel number message 1010 as just a coincidence, pay more attention because it has a deeper meaning in your life. Your angels are hoping that you will sit up, take notice, and decipher the message that they want to convey.

The angel number 1010 also invites you to be more courageous about your choices. Step out of your comfort zone. See what the rest of the world has to offer.

It also denotes spiritual enlightenment and awakening. You will find that by maintaining a positive attitude and a cheerful disposition, you are also attracting the positive energies of love.

The meaning of number 1010 is to keep a happy spirit in good times, and even in bad times also. Easier said than done. Imagine just how much positive energy you will be attracting.

The number 1010 encourages you to seek help from your angels because they will not hesitate to come to your aid. They are just a prayer away. They want to work with you.

You are responsible for the life you create, so make sure it is worth everybody's while. Live a life that would make anybody wish they had yours. Be the light.

The angel number 1010 is the number of beginnings and the number of endings. The end is never really the end. When one door closes, another opens, and it is usually better and more exciting. Make sure that you are opening a lot of doors. Keep your thoughts positive, and make sure your soul mission is your primary focus. Live a life of intent and attract the abundance you deserve.

Know that anything is possible for you right now. You can believe in the skills and the gifts that you can achieve the impossible. Dream big and see yourself achieving it. You do not lose anything by dreaming. If you want to make this dream come true, you can put your trust in divine guidance and in your strengths and abilities. They should share the equal load. Nothing will be accomplished if all you do is hope and pray. You will also not find fulfillment in achieving your goals if you are not in tune with your spirit.

Angel number 1010 wants to reassure you. You will achieve success in all your experiences. Now is the best time to start trying new things and take on exciting projects.

Do not be afraid to venture out into the unknown. Getting out of your comfort zone is one way you can grow and achieve personal fulfillment.

The angel number 1010 reminds you that you have the power to create your reality with your thoughts and actions. Make sure that you focus on thoughts that can help you attain your life purpose. You do not want it the other way around.

It is the beginning of a very enlightening journey. Enjoy the ride. Your best life is about to happen.

## PART 12: WHAT DOES THE UNIVERSAL / ANGELIC NUMBER MESSAGE 1111 MEAN?

Another universal number message is 1111. 1111 is the number message of ascended masters who impacted humanity and shifted the vibrations of our earth throughout history. The ascended masters, like Buddha, Jesus Christ, and Quan Yin, are sending you the message that you are a divine agent of the Creator as master at being yourself in human form. You are being reminded that you came here to make Earth a better place for future generations. Remember, you can make a positive difference in the lives of many or change the world for just one person. Seeing 11:11 is the trigger to set you on your path to make a mark in this existence. The world is grateful to have you!

Just as with all universal number messages, also known as angelic number messages, it is crucial to pay attention to your surroundings. Carefully sense what 11:11 means to you. The message for 11:11 is the same message for 1:11.

# PART 13: WHAT DOES THE UNIVERSAL / ANGELIC NUMBER MESSAGE 1212 MEAN?

Another universal/angelic number message is 1212. Repeatedly seeing 1212 everywhere is a divine sign and not a coincidence, as you might think. According to Merkabah mysticism, 12:12 is a code portal. When you enter in resonance with it, your Merkabic field is activated. When this happens, you are in alignment with the human heart connecting to the Unity Consciousness. When you see 1212, you are connecting to the golden light of Christ energy which will awaken divine love within you and activate new energy frequencies to help you evolve with the New Earth.

In Numerology, 1212 offers you the needed energy to transform your key relationships. Hence, from this perspective, seeing 1212 is a message to you about being ready to better the significant connections in your life. Keep in mind, the individuals you choose to surround yourself with impact the way you think, act, and feel. When you see 1212, it is a reminder to build bonds with people who have a higher energetic level than you, so you can surround yourself with those who can influence your future and help you carry out your life's mission. Overall, be with people who inspire you, push you, and encourage you to dream bigger.

Seeing 1212 means stepping out of your comfort zone and starting anew in your life. You begin pushing yourself towards something different because your soul always knows what is best for you at any given moment. It is nudging you to take action which is in alignment with your highest truths about yourself. For this reason, your angel message is about having the faith and courage to take a step into unchartered waters, and as your path unfolds, you will discover what is being revealed to you is far greater than anything you ever imagined. Trust that you are safe.

There are three other important spiritual meanings and reasons of why you are seeing 1212. The first meaning of 1212 is you are on the right track. Even if circumstances may appear like you are on the wrong path, the truth is that you are really on the right path.

For example, Thomas Edison, usually credited for the invention of the light bulb, had one thousand failed experiments before they invented it. In Edson's words, "I did not fail one thousand times. The light bulb was an invention with one thousand steps."

Go through it one step at a time. You are starting to see solutions show up in your life because you have shifted frequencies to align yourself with the desired outcome for your highest good. Your life is moving in the direction you did not see coming, and the blessings are phenomenal.

The second meaning of the message 1212 is to keep a positive state of being. Be aware of your thoughts. Our thoughts create our reality. Reach your highest potential with positive thoughts.

Being grateful for what you have is a sure way to keep a positive mind. You attract more success and abundance into your life when you are thankful. Focus on what you have, not what you do not have.

"Watch your thoughts; they become words. Watch your words; they become actions. Watch your actions; they become habits. Watch your habits; they become character. Watch your character; it becomes your destiny." - Lao Tzu.

The third meaning of 1212 is manifesting your dreams by the power of thought.

Wishes are like seeds. They provide the fuel that propels actions. Not doing anything leads to nothing. You need to be willing to do what it takes to make your wish come true by doing something towards achieving your wish every day. If your thoughts and action are out of alignment, your desires cannot be fulfilled. Everything that currently exists in your life was once a wish.

In the big picture, the Universe is like one giant tapestry with colorful woven threads where each thread represents a human life. It is an example of how your life is interwoven, crossing, and touching all the other lives until every human being is affected. We are all represented in the tapestry. Just like teamwork, we all intertwine and influence each other.

Seeing 1212 is a message of divine unity. Make new connections and share your gift with the world. Be a changemaker - the Universe supports you!

# PART 14: WHAT DOES THE UNIVERSAL / ANGELIC NUMBER MESSAGE 1234 MEAN?

The last angelic number message I will mention is 1234. If you are repeatedly seeing the message 1234, this is no coincidence at all. Nothing happens by chance.

1234 means simplify your life and start fresh. Additionally, seeing this number quite often could be an angel message from a higher realm. This message tells you about your awakening and coming back to your true self.

The one thing to keep in mind when you see 1234 or 123 repeatedly is there are several different meanings. It is essential for you to observe what 1234 means to you. As a start, I will now let you know three common spiritual meanings and reasons of why you are seeing 1234 everywhere.

The first meaning of 1234 is the magic of spiritual decluttering to reach clarity. It is time to simplify your life. This can refer to decluttering around you as well as within you. It is time to let go of the past and move forward in your life journey.

Remember this, seeing 1234 signifies the releasing of excess baggage, whether it is mental, emotional, or physical, so you can make room in your "earthly suitcase" to pack all the right items to make your life journey amazing. Giving yourself importance and clearing your environment can open a path to positive energy so you can obtain clear thinking for your life purpose. Make this life count and move towards a new you!

*"You cannot reach for anything new if your hands are still full of yesterday's junk."* – Louise Smith.

The second meaning of 1234 is you are on the right track to finding your life purpose.

The Universe is communicating to you all the time, and you need to be tuned in to receive the message and understand the signs. When you hear the Infinite Creator's call, it is your choice if you choose to listen.

When you see 1234, you know you are on the right track of your life mission. The reason is that 1234 represents a number sequence of digits that are moving upwards in their order, like steps on a ladder. Taking steps to find the right path in life is like finding your way through a maze. You take one step at a time in the direction that you feel is right for you, and if that path does not work out, you try a different path until you finally find the exit. There is nothing to fear because each step you took was a step towards your goal.

It is a reminder you are taking steps to reach your soul's purpose, and it is perfectly unique just for you. Remember this always, you have the choice to change the direction of your path anytime in the way that brings you the most happiness. All you can do is take the first step in the present moment. Trust in divine timing. You are capable of greatness!

The third meaning of 1234 is your real well being comes from internal achievement. 1234 is a combination of concepts associated with self-determination, exploration, independence, teamwork, and creativity. It is related to becoming a better person by developing new and better ways to be your true self, taking positive action to do things that are good for you, and gaining knowledge and wisdom from experiences so you can learn more about yourself and attain inward health.

The number message 1234 signifies great experience because it comes in full circle, it starts from 1 and comes back to 1, when you add up all the digits. Although it speaks of being self-determined and independent from others, after going through all the stages of development, you have achieved human leadership qualities. These qualities include positivity, purpose, empathy, compassion, humility, and love that guides and motivates others to be better humans. As a result, you are respected by the people around you. In return, you are happy because you feel satisfied and good about yourself. You are rich internally. It is this achievement that echoes through time and can bring real blessings for the future world.

Remember to embrace the need for continual improvement. The goal in life is to develop our highest potential, to be responsible in your present life, and understand the law of cause and effect. For every action, there is an equal and opposite reaction. Your thoughts, words, and actions ignite waves of energy throughout the Universe which result in desirable or undesirable manifestations. Your good thoughts, words, emotions, and actions are important for a better world.

What should you do next when you see 1234? Taking the first step toward your soul's urge will set you in the direction of your highest potential. Even if you make a mistake, it is the best way to figure out where you are going.

When you are seeing 1234 often, it is a reminder that you are on the right track toward your life purpose, and the entire Universe supports you. You care more about living in alignment with your soul's truth, and you realize that your purpose is about being love. Your goal is to make a difference and leave something for the next generation.

Whether you have contributed to a scientific breakthrough or created a new product, the impact can reach well beyond your lifetime. However, helping people also counts as something that will outlast the duration of your existence, because you are improving not just their lives, but the lives of all the other people they have been in contact with you. This is the greatest gift you can give to the future.

Live the life beyond yourself, and be kind, caring, and giving. Most importantly, be patient when building something that will last beyond your lifespan to improve the existence of humankind. It is your turn to change the world!

# CHAPTER 11: WHAT ARE THE PURPOSES OF THESE MESSAGES?

A s you have just learned, there are many universal/angelic number messages. There are numerous other universal/ angelic number messages out there, but I feel these are the most pertinent number messages. You have learned about 000 through 999, 1010, 1111, 1212, and 1234.

I want to share my wisdom with these number messages, so they will motivate and inspire you like they have with me. They are the silver linings amongst the clouds. When you are given lemons, make lemonade. These number messages may also motivate and inspire you during the most amazing times in your life as well. Remember, it is not a coincidence you see these numbers. My favorite saying is there is no such thing as a coincidence. My other favorite saying is that everything happens for a reason.

# CHAPTER 12: HOW SOME OF THESE MESSAGES RESONATED WITH ME

## PART 1: 222

I just saw 2:22 on the clock. I am going to now share how this universal/angelic message resonates with me and my thoughts just now, so you can see an example of how this message may resonate with you. There are several messages with universal/angelic messages. They may affect us differently, so these messages are based on your personal thoughts when you see one of these messages. These messages are very inspirational for me as I hope they will be for you as well.

222 is commonly related to the beginning of expansion that reflects growth in a certain area of your life. When I saw 2:22 this time I was thinking about how I am significantly healing from the

past, so I can be more present. 2:22 resonates because I am healing significantly and growing from the work I am doing, when it comes to getting rid of excess baggage.

Almost right after I saw this 2:22 message I saw an anonymous quote on a Facebook post. "Damaged people are dangerous because they know how to survive." This is synchronicity.

## PART 2: 999

Another message I saw today is 999. This is a message I rarely see. I cannot even remember if I even saw this message before. I was so excited, so I pulled into a parking lot to look up the message of 999. The message of 999 means something in your life is ending or will be completed soon. I have recently been ending this chapter in my life. Perfect synchronicity with receiving confirmation from the Universe and angels.

## PART 3: 1010

The universal/angelic number message 10:10 assisted me. I will let you know an example, so you can see how the number message 10:10 may also assist you. I am cleaning my side of the street, so to speak, with contacts, and I started getting frustrated. I turned around, and the clock had 10:10 on it. I know I will be ok and even stronger as time goes on no matter what because the universe has my back according to the universal/angelic number message 10:10. Seeing this message is very comforting.

# PART 4: 12:12

I will now share an example of what happened when I saw 12:12 just now. Hopefully this will assist you when you happen to see 12:12 anywhere. 12:12 is a message to let you know your life is moving in a direction that you did not see coming, and the blessings are phenomenal. I love surprises because the universe and my Higher Self always have my highest good in mind. I went back to my phone after I saw 12:12, and I saw a quote on Facebook that applies with the 12:12 message. The quote is "Sometimes you have to let go of the picture of what you thought it would be like and learn to find joy in the story you are living," by Rachel Marie Martin. How is that for synchronicity?

# CHAPTER 13: WHAT IS THE NEXT STEP OF HEALING?

I am so glad you are wondering the next step in healing. Healing can be so fun when you put a positive spin on it. We are all works in progress. It is always important to put yourself first. This is looked at as being selfish, but this is the healthy route. Just think when you are healthy, you can make healthy choices as to who you choose as your soulmates or your twin flame. If you are unhealthy, you may not make such healthy choices. This is not being selfish, your soulmate or even your twin flame will thank you. You can learn more about soulmates and twin flames in chapter 14. We all need human contact. Once you are healed, you may meet one of your soulmates or even your twin flame. If you are already in a relationship, your partner may be one of your soul mates or even your twin flame. The healing will only cause the relationship to improve, but it may be a bumpy road. Relationships take work, but they are so worthwhile when you find an amazing mate. in this case. As you will learn about in chapter 14, you have multiple soulmates, but one true twin flame. You will learn about this now as you read chapter 14.

# SECTION 6: SELF-LOVE AND LOVE OF OTHERS

# CHAPTER 14: TWIN FLAMES
# AND SOULMATES

N ow that we have seen the messages of universal/angelic number messages and worked on ourselves, let us find out about love of others. What are twin flames? What are soulmates? What is the difference between twin flames and soulmates? Keep reading.

## PART 1: WHAT IS A TWIN FLAME?

Twin flames, also called twin souls, are literally the other half of your soul. We each have only one twin, and generally after being split the two went their separate ways, incarnating over and over to gather human experience before coming back together. Ideally, this happens in both of their last lifetimes on the planet so they can ascend together, so you probably have not had many lifetimes with your twin.

Each twin is a separate soul, not half a soul. It is their task to become more whole, balancing the female and male sides, and ideally becoming enlightened, before reuniting with their twin. This reunion is of two complete and whole beings. All other relationships through all our lives could be said to be practice for the twin because this is the ultimate relationship.

## PART 2: WHAT IS A SOULMATE?

Soulmates are our soul family, the ones we do have many lifetimes and experiences with, who help us grow and evolve, create, and dissipate karma. According to ancient wisdom, when the soul is born or descended from Source, it is created in a group. The souls in this group are our soulmates, ones who are very like us in frequency makeup. Then each of these souls is split into two, creating the twins.

A soulmate is someone you are close to at a soul level, and with whom you had many shared experiences in different lifetimes. Soulmates exist in various kinds of relationships, such as siblings, parent-child, best friend, as well as romantic relationships. There is a deep love for each other, and a spiritual bond that sets them apart from the superficiality of most other people in your life. Conversations are generally deep about personal growth and service to make the world a better place. We can have many soulmates in our lives, and they come to us to help us grow spiritually.

# PART 3: PERSONAL EXPERIENCES WITH POSSIBLE TWIN FLAMES AND SOUL MATES

When I was going to high school, I was walking towards a gentleman and he was walking towards me. We were both headed to the same hallway. I fell in love at first sight. Later I was with a contact who happened to be friends with the gentleman, and I was unexpectedly at the gentleman's father's home. He walked up to me and told me we saw each other at school. I had a block on my memory, so I could not remember. He started persisting, but the memory was not coming back to me. It was not until recently that I recalled seeing him at school and locking eyes. He called me flame at his father's house another time I was there. He recognized me. When he called me flame face to face in front of me, I gained my confidence back, stood up straight, and said yes. I recognized him also. At that time, I was dating our mutual friend. He insisted I stay with our friend, but he wanted to be friends. When I was walking home from high school, he would end up coming across me as I was just around the corner from where I lived. He would drive me home from there. I thought that was so cute. He is one of the only people who ever called me flame. We have recently reconnected with our energy. I feel his energy around me often. I do not know what the future holds with him yet. We think about each other often though.

Soulmates can be other souls other than significant others. Soulmates can be family like animals too. My cat, Rockstar, is a soulmate. I call him Rockstar because he keeps me going. He is my rock. He is my foundation. He is a star because he plays a huge role in my life, and he is of the Universe. When I was younger, I planned for this time in my life. I planned to meet a cat that is an outdoor cat, and who is an orange and white or black and gray tabby. I wanted a male cat because for the most part males have always been more affectionate with me. This description describes Rockstar down to every detail. I met him about a year and a half ago. He was an outdoor kitten before he lived with me. I brought him into my apartment from a family who kept him outdoors. He needed a better home. The day after I had him live with me in my apartment. It was one of the coldest days of that winter. The local schools were closed due to extremely cold temperatures. I did not know this ahead of time. This is called Divine timing because I saved him from freezing outdoors. He may not have survived. Rockstar and I are very in tune with each other. When I went through Dark Nights of the Soul recently, he provided pet therapy. I was stuck in bed at certain times, and he did wellness checks by joining me in bed and checking on me. He knew I was not doing well. I am telepathic and communicate with animals. He came out when he saw I am home. We were glowing and smiling from ear to ear. Nothing comes between Rockstar and me. The Universe is on the side of Rockstar and me. We make an amazing team!

Butch is another cat that is a soulmate of mine. He lived with me when I was younger. I saw a newspaper clipping about a cat needing a good home. I read the newspaper article, and I am intuitive and pointed to the newspaper clipping as I exclaimed, "This is the kitten!" I was ecstatic! We went to where he was living. I was introduced to the mother cat and the litter of kittens. Butch was outside playing in the mud. Butch came inside just then and peeked around the corner of the wall. I was glowing, and so was Butch. Then he hid behind the railing of the staircase that was across the room from me. We played peek-a-boo. We were both smiling and glowing. Then Butch ran up to me and jumped into my lap. I was highly allergic, so I hid my face in his fur so my allergies would not show. I was asked if I am allergic. I lied, and I told her I am not allergic. We took Butch home with us. Butch and I are also very in tune with each other. When he was in the car with me, I put the cat carrier on my lap. There is a song, by The Four Tops, with the lyrics, "Baby, I need your loving." I changed the words to "Butch, I need your loving." I would sing to him. This calmed him as he put his chin in my hand and fell asleep. My singing was not bad, so it was not because he was bored, rather relaxed. At night, Butch would get scared from the raccoons and possums outdoors. He would cry. I would call him to me. He would hear me and respond. Then I would respond. We took turns talking to each other as he found me in bed. I was asked what I am doing. I replied that I am talking to Butch. He would find me and jump into bed with me. He would play in my hair until we both relaxed and fell asleep. I outgrew the allergies by forcing myself to become immune due to the love I have for him. Love can overcome anything. Butch passed away when I was a teenager. I sense spirits, and I swear Butch visits me sometimes. We are that close.

Another animal that is my soulmate is Biscuit. Biscuit is a dog I had when I was younger also. She was a police dog, so she was very well trained. She was a golden retriever. She and I would glow around each other just like Butch and I did. Biscuit also passed away when I was a teenager. I know for a fact she visits me to this very day. I glow every time I know she is with me. She glows also. We tend to glow around the same time.

Another example of a soulmate or possible twin flame, depending on what the future holds is, is written about below. I had always intuitively known since I was a young kid that I would meet a man named Pete. Pete is not his real name, but I will use the name Pete in this example. I was tested for being gifted as a kid, and it turns out I am. This is how I knew about Pete since I was a kid. Then one day Pete was at an acquaintances home. My friend and I needed a ride home, so he drove me home. On the way we kept gazing into each other's eyes in the rearview mirror. I was seventeen at the time. I always thought we would meet when I was fifteen or so. We keep running into each other from out of nowhere. I have not seen him in about three years now. We end up getting together on and off. We have so much in common. It is hard to imagine I have this much in common with someone. When he found out about my intuition test in third grade, he smiled from ear to ear. I miss him a lot. We are always energetically connected.

I could write about my soulmates all day because I have numerous soulmates, but those are some of my soulmates who have made a huge impact on my life thus far. They are considered my soul family. One never truly knows what the entire future holds. Hopefully these examples give a closer look as to a possible twin flame and soulmates.

# PART 4: REAL TWIN FLAME SIGNS

Twin flames are very rare. Soulmate karmic connections are more common. Twin flames are becoming a lot more prevalent. Before you were born, you had two parts kind of like ying and yang. You have the divine masculine part, and you have the divine feminine part. When you are born, your soul splits in half, you have the divine masculine and the divine feminine. Your one soul was split apart into two different people.

Some people are like well what if I am gay. Two parts of your soul can incarnate into the same sex. One soul will take on traits of the divine masculine. The other soul will take on traits of the divine feminine, so you can be gay and have a twin flame.

Twin flame relationships get confused all the time for soulmate and karmic relationships which is understandable. The relationship is intense and real. Keep reading to learn about signs that are only true for twin flame relationships.

There is no such thing as a coincidence. When you meet it will be very serendipitous. It is surreal and perfect. Your twin flame can meet you anywhere. Your twin flame will come into your life from out of nowhere. The way you meet will be serendipitous.

Before you meet him or her, you will be picking up hobbies you never picked up before. You may dream about him or her anywhere from two years to two months before you meet your twin flame. The hobbies you pick up that you did not pick up before are their hobbies. Your soul is getting prepared. Your soul will know he or she is coming. There will be some sort of foreshadowing. When you do get in contact with your twin you will feel completely comfortable around him or her. You may have your guard up because everyone comes with baggage, but ultimately you will feel very much at ease with him or her. You will feel you can fall asleep on him or her and not feel weird about it. Then when you get into a relationship with him or her you will feel some quirks, he or she has is the same quirks you have. It will be like looking into the mirror for the first time.

Similar past experiences will be shared. Some things that seem coincidental are not. The past for both you and him or her will be very aligned, and you two will have a very similar past.

Once you two start to get past the honeymoon phase past baggage will really start to come out. He or she will bother you in ways nobody has ever bothered you before. He or she will start to make you feel things you never felt before. He or she will make you angrier than anyone has ever made you angry before because he or she is a mirror reflection of yourself. He or she can pick at you and bother you, not in a way where you do not like him or her, but in a new way that really makes you face yourself. He or she will shine a light on who you really are and the things you have been trying to hide like your shadow self. There will be a lot of synchronicities like the universal/angel number messages I mentioned in section five.

When you are together different electrical occurrences will happen. This is because your energy is so powerful that it disturbs the lights. You will see the light flickering a lot when you are together. Road lights may go out. Loud ringing in your ears at high frequency levels will occur that you never heard before. These are signs from the angels that this is your twin flame.

You may have the same facial features. This does not mean you two will exactly look alike, but there will be similar smiles and gestures. There will be a very twin-like presence with you two. There will be something similar with the way you two move.

Despite what you think, you two will be very opposite. This is because one of you is the ying and one of you is the yang. One of you is the divine masculine, and one of you is the divine feminine.

You two will be very different. Your differences will complete each other. One of you may be more talkative, while the other is quieter. One of you may be more detail-oriented, while the other is big picture oriented.

It will be a mistake to feel you two are identical because you two are also quite opposites completing each other. Your strengths are his or her weaknesses. Your weaknesses are his or her strengths. You two will be an unstoppable force.

The things you two do have in common is the same core values, and what you both want in life. You two will want the same thing out of life. Both of you will have the same drive. Both of you will have the same values. This is what is important. Both of you will be opposites that balance each other, but at the same time, both of you will have the same core values and same drive.

Twin flames often have a huge age difference of up to ten years and longer, but at least ten years. We do not incarnate in synchronicities. This could be why there is such a huge age difference.

He or she will be your spiritual catalyst. You may be very spiritual, but once you meet your twin flame you will evolve in ways you have never evolved. You will get into manifesting your dream. You will get into your Higher Self. You will become your best self. When you meet your twin flame, this will help you grow in ways you have never grown before spiritually and as a person very rapidly as well. Due to this, you will fulfill a higher purpose.

With a twin flame it is not all about being in love or finding your other half. Your twin flame is here with you to change the world. Twin flames have a higher purpose in this world to make the world a better place. You two will raise the vibration together for the collective conscious, and you two will awaken people. You two will work very well together with a higher purpose, something to help humanity. This could be you are in the same business together. This could mean you both do charity work. Both of you will work well. The purpose of twin flames is to assist humanity, not a selfish reason of falling in love. That is the reason more twin flames are coming together. You both will have the same spiritual mission. You both will work very well together, and with following your true mission.

If you think someone is your twin flame, but he or she is aloof to you, he or she is not your twin flame. He or she has done nothing but used you for selfish reasons like physical, money, or because he or she is alone. If when you two first met there was not the same in tune feeling, then he or she is not your twin flame. If someone is your twin flame but keeps treating you wrong or keeps running away because there is a runner-chaser dynamic with twin flames, it is not in time to be with your twin flame, and you need to leave him or her alone and do more soul development because he or she can seriously hurt you.

Do not go chasing after your twin flame. If he or she is not ready, leave him or her alone to grow more. Do not stay in an awful relationship. It is better to leave him or her alone to grow instead of festering in an unhealthy relationship.

## PART 5: THE THREE CLASSIC FALSE TWIN FLAME CHARACTERISTICS

The sooner you can diagnose if he or she is a false twin flame the better. It takes time to heal.

1. One of the lovers is not in his or her Power. One is holding back. One is hiding these powerful events either from you or you from them because there is a deep seeded fear that one is powerful, so you are going to run. If one is constantly running when one steps into his or her power, the other feels threatened. In a twin flame relationship, they are both lifting each other up. You are true healers. A characteristic is if you are letting someone talk down to you. Sometimes this happens, but not all the

time. If you are constantly having to play it small, that is not a twin flame relationship.

2.  Your false twin flame stays if he or she gets to be your energy vampire. The person only stays if you heal them. If someone is depressed, and you cheered them up that is a codependent relationship, not a twin flame relationship. Maybe someone is going through a career crisis, you help them financially. You give them your light and advice. Invest your energy into your soul purpose. Do not use the energy for that one person. Use it on more quality people. Twin flames are healers. We are here to enlighten. First, we should heal ourselves, and then do purpose work. Then work with the beloved. When a healer feels someone is only into him or her for his or her healing asset it is not twin flame love. If you are feeling unworthy beyond healing qualities, look at it. If you are constantly chasing the person, this is not a twin flame. This is a codependent relationship. Look at that. Let him or her know that he or she can heal himself or herself instead of you doing it for him or her. If they get excited by that great. If not, he or she is not a twin flame. If he or she was with you to validate their ego that is a narcissist. That is not a twin flame. This is someone to avoid. You can call a twin flame in at your level when you put yourself and your purpose first. Someone will love you for who you, not how you heal him or her or what you give him or her.

A classic example is she falls in love with a guy who treats her like an energetic doormat. He takes, and she is in love, and does not notice. He stops returning her texts. Narcissists do the doormat treatment. Always set healthy boundaries. If you are too generous, you do not feel good enough about yourself. Raise your self-esteem, or you will constantly attract narcissists.

3.  False twin flames will put energetic hooks that look like energy cords in you, especially in the power center, heart chakra, and sexual chakra. When he runs, you may think he is a twin flame and in the runner phase. We may still feel connected because the energy cords. Get a psychic cord cutting. We only get corded because there is a wound. We do not need to be attached. We can be individuals.

## PART 6: COMING INTO REUNION WITH YOUR TWIN FLAME

Twin flame reunions are the most fulfilling relationships we can have as humans on all levels. However, twin flame couples have been extremely rare on the planet, and for good reasons. Despite this, we are finding that more twins are finding each other now because of the acceleration of spiritual transformation and opportunities for soul evolution we are all experiencing. People are evolving, learning, and healing at such a fast rate that they are getting ready for their twins faster. What used to take lifetimes to learn and heal, people are now going through in years or even months. This is the amazing level of acceleration we and the planet are going through.

When twins reunite, it is for spiritual service work. Due to this, the union is a huge birthing of creative energy released to be used for their mission together. More twins are attempting to get together now to help the planet and humanity make a big shift forward in consciousness.

Many of these attempts at reunion are unsuccessful because the individual people are not quite ready for the intensity of a twin flame union. It is more intense than any other union, and this intensity is at soul level, not as much in the physical or even emotional bodies. This does not mean that there is not a good attraction at those levels as well, but the strongest attraction is of spirit. This is one of the distinguishing characteristics of a twin soul. Many people think they have met their twin because the attraction is so intense, but it is a karmic attraction, one of need or desire that is unique of the divine love of twins.

Your chance of meeting and staying with your twin depends on how much of your baggage from this and past lives you have cleared. The biggest reason twins need to separate after going together is their individual emotional baggage. In the presence of your twin, there cannot be anything between you, nothing blocking your closeness. This means that everything comes up for healing which you have not previously healed.

When twins reunite both experience an acceleration of their spiritual growth and awakening. They get on the fast track of learning about esoteric wisdom and experiencing other states of consciousness. They usually have not been together all that often during their series of lives on the planet, and their backgrounds may be different. Yet, there is a closeness and similarities of spirit that are almost uncanny and noticed in many ways, such as looking back at yourself when you look at your mate, and a remembering of the distant past when you first split up. Guidance is strong with these relationships, and usually one or both have a good channel for communication with Spirit. Their connection is telepathic and hugging each other is like coming home for nourishment.

## PART 7: EVENTS OF A TRUE TWIN FLAME

The intensity of connection causes it to feel surreal. The souls and intuition will know if this is a twin flame bond. There are things that apply only to a twin flame bond. The bond is more intense than soulmates. Twin flames have always been connected since we were created. This applies to souls in spirit form or in human form. Some feel they are always connected to someone with inner knowing, but they do not know who this person is though.

A lot of times we will be presented with a catalyst. Soul contracts come into play here. Intensity and endurance builds for twin flames. A catalyst will shake your life up, and a catalyst will give you heartache and pain for true connection with twin flame.

Many have dreams about the twin flame before meeting them. They will feel an energetic shift and presence. They feel energy before meeting them. There is soul recognition. There are feelings of coming home, infinity, and feelings of this lasting for an eternity. There are feelings of coming back to the tribe. Twin flames have the soul signature with them. They have unconditional love, honor, respect, and trust. Essentially, we are one. We are the essence. There is instinctual initial consciousness. Twin flames are one. We may not know, but our higher selves know. Many synchronicities happen before meeting one's twin flame also. After meeting, a sign is synchronicity. What you are experiencing is significant. You are on your path. Synchronicities confirm significance of what we are experiencing.

There are similarities with dates, such as birth dates, as well as family structure, family dynamics, and the way we grew up. Experiences are parallel. There are similarities with physical traits, gifts, personalities, and abilities. This is because we are a unit, and we share the same soul essence. Yes, we are separate souls and have our own individualities. There are similar interests, such as music, arts, nature, and medicine. Twin flames mirror each other. They have the same essence. There are similar interests, goals, and passions. There is a deep soul resonance.

After the love bubble, we experience disruptions. This is another sign. Work needs to be done. Work with energy by mirroring. It can be painful due to love between twins. Mirroring can become too intense. We trigger our twin flame. We love each other subconsciously, emotionally, mentally, and soulfully. There is very deep unconditional love.

No one can trigger our twin flames the way we do, or the way we can. For example, one day you may be talking to your twin and tell him or her you are so grouchy, so mean. When in solace, your twin's words come up and you start to question. The twin will ask himself or herself why she or he is a grouch. This could be due to childhood experiences. The train of thought tries to figure it out. You start to blame others. This goes deep to the root. The trigger was not only an emotional stir, but it also became a deep-rooted emotional barrier. It is something that needed to be addressed. Purging can be intense due to this. Separation can be necessary. A lot of us construe separation as a negative. We may feel they do not appreciate us. Maybe he or she went off with a soulmate. Maybe he or she got married and cannot let go. That is how it is displayed in the third dimension. Separation and running on a higher level can be healing. Twin flames balance each other. They become a union. They can hold a physical union. They are polarities coming into a true union. Sometimes it takes time to balance. Then we see each other again. Then there may be separation again. There could be back and forth for a little while. Higher aspects begin to merge. Instead of the connection growing weaker, it gets stronger and more powerful. Although the twin may be married and not want to talk, we are still becoming closer and closer together. There is still merging and going through deeper merging. We are not pulling away. We are becoming closer. This is a huge indication.

Although there can be a deep connection with a soulmate or someone you date, if you ever experience a break up, it only grows weaker, not stronger. This is not a twin, so you go your own ways. It may hurt for a bit, but you grow stronger after.

There is no sensing energy. There is no synchronicity. Even if there is, the connection grows weaker. It has no fuel. It just dies.

The connection with twin flames grows more powerful and deeper. Only twin flames will be a constant connection. Only twin flames can ignite your alchemical process for deeper more spiritual transformation.

You may have a soulmate you love and care for that pushes you to become a better person in the third dimension. They may push you to accomplish things, to gain material things, become a better person, but you hit a wall. A twin flame will not only cause you to become a better person, but anything that has been buried and needs to surface will be transformed. Your twin flame forces you to bring up things you need to deal with. This is a main sign. They cause you to transform for the long run. They cause you to heal for the long run.

Others may try to get rid of your negative tendencies. They will not help you to heal like a twin flame can. This is the difference between twin flames and others.

After purging, transforming, mirroring, and things like that, the synchronicities continue to let you know confirmation, and you are on your path. You can communicate via your heart space. A soulmate can do this, but not heart to heart. This is only available to someone who is conjoint, like a twin flame, on all levels. This is through the heart center. This is the spark to want to do something, such as fulfilling the dream you want to fulfill. The twin flame will share the same. Dreams will become stronger. The visitations from your Higher Self become stronger. You start to feel your twin flame's Higher Self even more. You start to feel your twin flame's essence in the air. You start to get to know your twin's Higher Self in this reality before establishing a physical union. It becomes surreal. The bond will not cease. This is how you know it is your twin flame. It is like coming home to your twin. People can feel familiar, but not everybody can feel like home.

People misconstrue. It is not just about synchronicities or having a deep connection with someone. That is not enough. It is not just about having dreams of this person or seeing their name everywhere. It is not just about being in love with him or her. It is not just about breaking up with him or her. It is not just about being on and off again with this person. Going back and forth is unhealthy. It may be a twin flame, but not necessarily. Those things happen with any relationship. The difference between separating and coming back again with a twin flame is healthy because you are purging and healing with him or her.

When it is a soulmate the back and forth thing is not healthy because it is not only stressing you out, and you are not healing from it. You may purge and be triggered, but it is not deeply healing you, so you need to just let people go. Your twin flame is the energy behind it and healing you, not hurting you. Your twin flame will never hurt you soulfully. That is not to say some twin flames do not have karma or will not hurt you in the physical because they do. On a soul level they will not. If your twin flame is hurting you and intentionally hurting you, you need to analyze that. Maybe your twin flame is suffering from an attachment or an attack, or a manipulation. Your twin flame will never hurt you intentionally. It is not possible. It is not part of the dynamic. Evaluate your situation. Consult with your guides, your team, and with Source directly if you are enjoying it from a conscious space and an authentic space, in which you really are in dire need for some answers. Pray. Your team will give you the answers. Whoever does not belong in your life will make their way out of it one way or another. Always remember that.

# PART 8: TEN STAGES OF A TRUE TWIN FLAME JOURNEY

There are catalysts, twin flames, and false twin flames. A false twin is led through Spirit and misleads. Some believe in that, and some do not.

1. When you first meet your twin flame you will notice there is something about him or her. It is different than anybody who you ever met before. The initial meeting with this person is mutual. You could meet after missing a train or flight. If it is online, you instantly feel a connection and you do not know why. They come out of nowhere. It is as if they come from out of thin air.

2. There is a sense of familiarity on the first date. You feel like you have met the one. You may even question on how it can happen to be so real and so fast. It is a message your soul is sending your human form. There is unconditional love and recognition. It goes beyond

anything in the third dimension. The connection cannot be explained. It can be felt. You two are so connected, and it is so familiar, as if you two have known each other for years because you two have known each other for years. You have known him or her since the beginning of time. You have had multiple catalysts to prepare you for your twin flame. A huge sign is familiarity.

3.  You may notice physical mirroring situations like one is right handed maybe, and the other is left handed. You may have a mole on the left side of your face, while the other may have a mole on the right side of his or her face. Facially, you look very much like your twin. This does not have to be, but maybe your eyes, nose, and smile are similar. You two may be different ethnicities, religions, ages, genders, and social statuses. You two may be on the opposite side of the globe. This is done to help break down old paradigms of distance and separation because as we know the world has divided itself amongst color, sexual orientation, and age group status. The purposes of the twin flames to heal the world and bring those differences together. We can break down old third dimension paradigms.

4.  You two will usually meet on a synchronized date such as 11/11, 4/14, 7/17, 8/8, 8/18, and so on. Universal/Angelic number messages show up. You have a knowing that

something is going on. At this point, you are still confused a bit, but you notice something is going on which is bigger than the both of you. Your souls have awakened now, so it is time to have the awakening.

5. You will mirror each other exactly. Your twin flame will mirror your worst fears, and everything that comes up inside of you. In the third dimensional programming it will change out in the open. Often, we will blame our twin and ask how things changed so quickly when you thought you met the one. This is your ego fighting because it knows your souls know each other which means ascension. Your ego can not survive in the present. It can only survive in the past and in the future, so the ego needs to know what happened and what will happen as your soul goes with the flow. There is no fear with the soul. Egos recognize this. Fear, differences, and arguments start coming out now. You start thinking there must be something wrong here. This can last from a couple of months to a couple of years. You need to go through twin flame separation to feel this contrast.

6. You got through this pain and most dreadful separation. This is the runner-chaser dynamic that is often described with twin flames. One twin is always more awakened and seeming to want this connection more. This was agreed between the two before they were born that one

will awaken first. The feminine leads spiritually while the masculine leads physically. The feminine is usually the chaser and the masculine wants this energy because they do not know what just happened. The masculine usually gets afraid because he has more karma from other lives that he is trying to get rid of in this life, so that is why he or she runs. They are usually running from themselves, and they are not running from you. This is usually when you go through ego death and Dark Nights of the Soul. Everything that you care about is yanking you from your ego and pride. You feel like you are losing your mind. Your beliefs are challenged. You start to question your entire existence. You are confused, heartbroken, angry, sad, and even suicidal. Illnesses might come up. Your twin is not usually speaking to you at this point on a physical level. Others are telling you to move on, and others are telling you he or she is not the one. You start to question this because you have never felt this way about anyone. It is so intense. You just know there is something more to life than a small voice telling you to not give up. That is your soul telling you to be yourself and not your ego.

7. You have ascended to a certain level, but not quite awakened yet. You start to seek answers to what is going on because you keep feeling the pull, dreaming about him or her, and keep seeing 1111 and do not understand

why. Law of attraction comes into play. You start manifesting the life you always wanted. You get the urge to clean up life spiritually, mentally, and emotionally. You learn about feminine and masculine energies and how we all want to possess both. You usually embody both, but none more than the other. Your twin embodies both, but the other more, the one you do not embody as much. That is the polarization of ying and yang. The goal is to do this within yourself first, but that is why you meet your twin in the physical to get that wake-up call. That is why 1111 starts following.

8. Once you learn about the term twin flame, and he or she finds you randomly, you start researching it more and start finding out how it makes sense to your situation. You may still feel doubt at this point because you are still trying to figure it all out, but your soul and guides are guiding you to clarity. You are called to the path when the time is right and to different people who will help your soul to ascend. You will learn lessons to clear karma. When we are first awakening, it starts resonating.

9. You get the urge to do mission work and to learn the meaning of unconditional love, detaching, and letting go. You may also feel like studying tarot or other signs of energetic healing. You may also feel you develop psychic abilities you have never thought about or pushed away as

a child due to society. It is societal rules, and they say it is witchcraft and stuff society thinks are wrong like psychic abilities. We all have these abilities, but we are conditioned to keep it closed. The twin flames are lightworkers and this is our purpose for coming here. We also came here to help the planet ascend and carry out mission work. You are experiencing different dimensions and souls to help which is why psychic abilities start happening. You start seeing things for what they really are. You are guided by something higher.

10. You learn how to see through the third dimensional illusions, and the reason you met your twin flame is to love yourself for the future you, your soul, and how to ascend, so it is self-love versus self-love for our body. This is important, but it is also about loving your soul and your own company. You want to learn the third dimensional physical companionship with your twin flame is the final reward of your mission and being whole with your soul. You have a knowing you are being led to a greater and higher purpose, but you finally start to see physical changes in the world, around you, and in your own physical body. Then there are DNA upgrades and synchronicity. You learn how to move energy, like reiki. You just develop these skills to move energy, change your life physically, and know you are a powerful creator. You realize you are a multidimensional being and not just

your body. You learn how to control your ego and not just your physical life to change whether you have your 3D in the physical or not. You start to meet a lot of soul family and make plans to carry out mission work. You start to practice gratitude and living in harmony versus your ego and prideful self. You will feel at ease with your twin flame and let it unfold organically. When you get to a place, and your twin flame comes back or not, either way is when you know you are ready for physical reunion and have reached a self-love and wholeness.

There will be those doubts. We are a soul in a human body, so we will have these emotions. We are kind of really fitting in with ourselves. Give yourself the benefit of the doubt. Fall in love with your soul. Falling in love with your soul has nothing to do with the ego. Knowing our souls is precious. It is about protecting our souls. Your soul has been you without your body longer. You need to protect it and go through the changes and lessons.

Are you holding onto this person out of ego or a need, or are you holding onto this person because you know he or she is the twin flame and your soul knows how special this one happens to be? You need to give your twin flame space so he or she can evolve and grow the way he or she was meant to grow. This is the healthy path.

It will not happen overnight. If you are nowhere near this, do not get mad at yourself because that is not true. You are probably closer than you think. You may just be going through the motions.

# CHAPTER 15: WHAT IS THE DIVINE FEMININE?

Twin flames are divinely matched soulmates. We may have numerous soulmates, but there is only one twin flame for each soul. This is known as the divine feminine and divine masculine. Their energy needs each other.

## PART 1: WHAT IS THE DIVINE FEMININE?

The divine feminine has nothing to do with religions, mystical schools, or any person, place, or thing. The actual meaning of the divine feminine has become distorted and often lost. The divine feminine has nothing to do with gender. It has nothing to do with mothering or nurturing. This isolates them in a certain category of creation. This does not mean mothering and nurturing are not part of the divine feminine.

The divine feminine is much greater, more expansive, more inclusive of all creations and beings. The divine feminine is a cosmic principal of creation. It is the space, the intention, the awareness, the energy flow that comes from the very essence of all that is and enables all creation to come forth. It is infinite in its potential and infinite in its form.

For this to be, it cannot be essentially any particular form, any particular symbol, or any particular person. Now a person or place can emanate or express those energies and use those energies principally and powerfully in the creations whether it be now or a grander scale.

It can be the unfolding of a landscape or sacred sight, or a lay line in the planetary system, but the divine feminine transcends any of the singularity or aspects of those forms. It is in all those, but beyond all those, encompasses all those, and offers all those when you are in the awareness in the energy of the flow of the divine feminine.

It is an entirely different experience of the nature of existence, nature of being, of where you come from, and where your true power of true expression originates. From that place it is hard to describe. Anything that creates a symbol, an idea, or a concept around the divine feminine diminishes it into only an aspect of what it essentially is.

Instead of connecting it into a symbol, an idea, or a place, it is to open yourself to an experience of an awareness, a connection, and an infinite potential of creation beyond which you may have ever known, experienced, or most likely could have imagined that exists. Knowing is true empowerment and true creative potential. Nothing outside yourself can provide this for you. It is your birthright.

## PART 2: A WOMAN'S STORY OF HER TRANSPERSONAL EXPERIENCES WITH THE DIVINE FEMININE

I found a case study of a female named Kimmie who shares her transpersonal experience with the divine feminine. Dawn Marie Rabey did this case study. I found it online in her blog "Women's Stories of Their Transpersonal Experiences with the Divine Feminine". I am now about to write about what Kimmie shared with the person who interviewed her. This is a fascinating account of the Divine Feminine.

I never really identified with the Divine Feminine until recently. I have recently connected with a Goddess group, and I do feel a more flowing intuitive sense. A coworker had books on various Goddesses that you could work with. I started to work with them in my own life a little bit, and I was starting to feel into that. It was like, "Yeah, I trust that's a real thing." I could feel it. It was subtle, yet powerful.

I decided to work with the Goddess Kali to help me get out of my rut, get rid of the old, and get on with it. Working with her really accelerated my life. I was afraid of not being accepted as an energy worker. This experience with calling in the Goddess Kali seemed to shift a lot. That was my first bigger experience with a feminine force.

Kali catalyzed a releasing, a destruction, and a letting go, in quite a fast way of old energy that was holding me back, such as feeling small. You know, just not standing up in my light, knowing that I have a light but believing it is better to keep it on the sidelines a bit more, and not stand up fully in public and those kinds of things. I know I am highly creative, I know I am very intuitive, and these are my talents and gifts in the world.

The next big piece happened this past summer. I also do hairdressing, and I have been developing this holistic hairdressing practice. Hairdressing is like being at home. It feels very grounding. I keep returning to it because it feels like a simple offering that is very healing.

I have been developing a new way to do this work. I feel like I am evolving a new way to do this craft, which feels kind of amazing because it is a staple service in our world. I was doing a lot of imagining about evolving my hairdressing practice in my head, and as a side thing to grow my energy healing practice. The salon, which is a work and live in studio came up for sale. The owner was leaving. I thought I was not interested because it would take away from my healing practice. When I sat in meditation, the guidance that I was getting was letting me know this is the way to go. My guidance is telling me I need to integrate these things somehow, I need to make a space that is about the physical outer balance, the hairdressing and weaves in the inner energy healing. It is not one or the other. Our bodies are our spirits. We are here, in the physical, and we need to take care of it too. This feels like where I am being directed to go, so I trust this.

This guidance feels like a spirit guide, and it comes through as a voice and a feeling. It makes me feel calm, relaxed, and centered. It feels like it is coming out of my heart. This guide has a feminine sense. The connection is the strongest it has ever been now. I feel like, as my vibration gets higher, I can hear and see her more clearly.

The next day, after getting the news about the space coming up for sale, I went to a sound healing I had booked with a colleague. In that experience I saw a vision. I had a vision of the salon, and how I would occupy these upper floors. The door burst open and then a white Divine light came up into the upper floors of this space and went out the top, sort of like the crown chakra. White light shot out the top, and it was like the whole space was to be occupied by me, and the healing needed to go upstairs.

That divine light needed to go upstairs so that healing was happening on all levels, including the base levels, the more physical world such as hairdressing but using natural products and approaching people in a more sacred and revered way than just kind of like crazy man-handling of hair. I went to the person selling the salon, and I said, "Yes, I'll buy it." What happened next is the juicy stuff.

I went to the burning man festival a couple months ago. While there, my partner and I went to this eye-gazing workshop. We practiced looking into one another's eyes. We were looking for the different faces that we would see in our partner, and it was amazing. We both work with these kinds of things in our lives, so we took it a bit further after the workshop and started to research who these beings were within us. We saw it as one, like if I saw this is in him, that could also be a part of me. I could be projecting that onto him as we do in partnerships, and it could also be a part of him. We both would check because he is quite connected to his guidance as well. We worked with muscle testing to find out what these faces were.

The most pertinent thing was that one of the things he saw in me was this younger, very artistic young woman, like in her twenties, who was using her creative artistic self as her power, but not in a powerful way. It was not a healthy energetic, she kind of had an attitude, like a negative power over attitude with her creations.

That was his perception. I tuned into it. When I asked my inner beings about that, I recognized that in myself from an earlier point in my life. When I first started hairdressing that was how I got my power, that is how I thought I was special. I had gifts in creativity. I did not have to work hard. I was just very good at doing amazing and creative things, and I got a lot of love and attention for it. It is what made me important, inside of myself, and without that I was not interesting. I would kind of use it. I would play that card a lot in various ways. It was a distorted way of getting love. I think I had undone a lot of that at this stage, but there was still this thing living within me.

As I found her, I saw inwardly, this Grove of Divine Feminine energy. It was a Grove of trees with an opening, and in the open space there was this hugely powerful high spiritual vibration feminine circle; a circle of Divine Feminine Beings standing in a Grove of trees. They were not in bodies. They were beings of light, but they were all unique. They were standing physically in a circle.

The sense was, "Let her move into the circle". I heard, "That will shed from her. She'll be able to release this." I saw her go into the middle, and the light of that circle holding her. It was like layers of this sadness and whatever was holding was draining into the earth, and she was being free.

Then I saw her become who I feel like I am now and how I would have been so much happier if I had access to that silly, fun, silly, girl who was fourteen. I saw her having that fourteen-year-old experience that she needed, in this circle, in the Grove of trees.

Then I had this overwhelming sense that, "If you feel scared, you can intend that any woman at this festival who needs this can come into the circle". So, then everyone, all these energy fields came into this Grove and just started shedding. I felt this wave of clearing as all this self-image stuff released. I saw the spirit of all these women who were at the festival come in; they did not physically come in, their energy came in. There were people coming from all directions into the Grove, filling the circle of feminine forms, and letting go of everything. This circle of feminine forms, which resembled light energy fields, held them all.

Then I was in my body dancing, while I was in the Grove at the same time. The feminine energy is saying, "Look where we are, and look at where the Grove is" and I see the Grove is surrounding the business, it is surrounding the salon space and what will be the healing space and it is basically saying, "We are holding this, and everyone who walks through that door is in the Grove, and everyone that comes in is coming for healing, and as they shed hair, energy, whatever, they come into who they are becoming, every single person, even the mailman.

Now as I work, daily the Grove with these feminine beings is guiding me. If I am feeling out of alignment, if I am feeling irritated, grumpy, judgmental, or stressed while I am in the act of doing my job, I connect with the Grove. I connect with the circle and the Grove, and I say, "Ok, what is actually happening here? Am I projecting, is this person just showing me something I need to heal, and what is this?" When I really need Source, if I am feeling disconnected or exhausted, I connect with the Grove, and this seems to help keep me aligned and in my heart. I feel like it is a huge amount of support, and it is like having a team of Divine Beings helping me. It is very amazing.

So here I am! That is my big Divine Feminine story unfolding right now was we speak. It is very wild. I am living it daily. It seems to be this Grove of Divine Feminine Beings is holding that for me.

# CHAPTER 16: DIVINE MASCULINE

J ust like there is a divine feminine, there is the counterpart, the divine masculine. You cannot have one without the other. Both the Divine Feminine and the Divine Masculine team together for the sake of ourselves, each other, and humanity. Our energy needs each other.

What is the Divine Masculine? Masculine energy is totally different from its counterpart. While the Feminine is inward directed, masculine is outward directed. Its characteristic is indeed movement. It is the kind of energy that moves from A to B and rushes forward to a goal. It does this through logic. The Masculine is right brain. This is good because logic and reasoning are tools needed to move through life, especially when it comes to planning and achieving goals. On our planet, this force has been disconnected from its real nature. The heart-mind connection has been cut causing us to live in a mind-driven society. We all have a third dimensional mind that separates and judges. We are here to clear it. That is why the Divine Masculine has not yet reached its full potential on Earth. The Divine Masculine is not patriarchal, ego based controlling energy that we call male. To awaken this God force, you need to bring all the energy you have stuck in your head back into your heart. The Divine Masculine and Divine Feminine need to reconnect. This will cause the male energy to flourish and express itself.

Another trait is the strength that comes from inside, from Spirit. Strength can make you go through the ascension journey challenges. The Divine Masculine will overcome all obstacles standing in the way. Man is a warrior, and he fights well. He fights for the truth for himself and others. He is the protector for the voiceless. He is linked with material abundance in the form of earthly needs. He is here to ensure abundance can flow easily.

Power is what allows the Divine Masculine to stand up for himself and for what is right. He has clearly defined boundaries that nobody can walk through. He is a King. He does not want to bend, bow, or kneel to anyone, and he does not want this from anyone. This is the inner power. This comes from knowing who you are. He is very determined. He uses focus with his determination. He will always reach for his dreams. He is resilient.

He embodies light. Light is information. He can easily connect to all that is. The Divine Masculine is a mystic and sage. He constantly is searching to improve, learn, and expand himself. He is the High Priest, and together with the Divine Feminine, who is the High Priestess, they hold the secret codes of the Mystery Schools needed to reach Divine Union and the highest level of ascension.

# CHAPTER 17: DIVINE FEMININE / DIVINE MASCULINE

B oth counterparts work together. They grow and heal together. Their energy needs each other. They balance each other.

## PART 1: HOW THE DIVINE FEMININE AND DIVINE MASCULINE WORK TOGETHER

The masculine protects and creates a safe space for the feminine. They want and need each other to birth at the same time. The Divine Masculine is the warrior. He says, "Do not fuck with me."

Culture is out of balance. Masculine is worshipped. It is time for the Divine Feminine to rise. For the Divine Feminine to continue to grow we need the Divine Masculine protector and space holder. Both the Divine Masculine and Divine Feminine need to rise to their highest potential together. The Divine Feminine may shut down if she does not have safety. They both need to feel protected. So, we may protect souls, hearts, and life force we must say, "Do not fuck with me," to those who are coming from unsafe places. "Do not fuck with me," protects innocent feminine energy.

The rise of the Divine Masculine and Divine Feminine together is important for the planet. We must cultivate the protector energy in all of us. To cultivate from a beginner level, practice saying no, speak up, and set boundaries. Ask your soul how you can be more courageous. Be more courageous.

To attract twin flames, you must have feminine energy and masculine energy. This is balanced ying and yang. To get a twin flame who is in tune, you must cultivate that within yourself. You must express in yourself what you want in your twin flame. We attract souls like ourselves.

It is important to see the light and be the light. This heightens consciousness. You will be a better light warrior when you cultivate your own self.

## PART 2: HOW TO AWAKEN THE DIVINE FEMININE AND THE DIVINE MASCULINE

The Divine Feminine and Divine Masculine are ying and yang. The Divine Feminine energy and the Divine Masculine energy lives within each of us. This is the union between these two energies. The greatest relationship you can have is with yourself. The Divine Masculine awakens by recognizing traits of the Divine Masculine. Every man on the planet is different. It is about becoming the greatest version of yourself. The Divine Masculine is about the protection and being a warrior for the community. The Divine Masculine is about upliftment of all of humanity. It is about sharing with the Divine Feminine too. There is an imbalance with the energy scales to put it lightly. It is very yang. People are desensitized. The masculine energy is direct and full of testosterone.

What makes the Divine Masculine divine? It is the ability for man to tap into their Divine Feminine. The two are related. Many artists gather inspiration from the hidden side of themselves, which is the Divine Feminine. They become empowered and better lovers.

The Divine Feminine can inspire the whole world in a split second. The Divine Feminine is about helping men rise to their higher nature. It is about nurturing the children of the world. The Divine Feminine is about embracing the beauty and reconnecting to the Divine Masculine. They are the warrior queens. They have phenomenal creativity and have awakened the warrior within themselves. They are the perfect fusion of right brain, which is creativity and left brain, which is logic. They do everything in response to each other. Gender is an illusion. Awakening these energies within ourselves frees us. The Divine Feminine has the power to get a man's heart going fast and hard. True beauty is unaware. When women see vulnerability there is no fear.

The Divine Feminine is not about competing with other women. It is about the sisterhood. Between your legs you have the stargate and portal from the unseen realms into the seen realms. These are the deep secrets. Sexuality is very sacred.

The Divine Feminine and Divine Masculine are complimentary. They work together to become one. Men and women surrender to each other. Right now, there are games, ownership, and pick up lines in too many relationships. At the same time, they block us from our authenticity. It is only when we tap into our authenticity that love can blossom. It is about letting go and not judging. When we awaken these principles from within, we create the perfect equilibrium. We see there is more to life. In higher realms, love takes on a whole new meaning. The Divine Feminine and Divine Masculine step in the cocreation they were meant to be, not just consumers. It is about generating energy, not taking energy.

The Divine Feminine and Divine Masculine can awaken at the same time because they have never been separated from one another. We do this by reconnecting back into ourselves, by going into nature, by fully embracing who we are by loving ourselves one hundred percent because there is no prototype of women or men. We are all vessels for life force to experience itself. We need to start breaking all the stereotypes

# SPECIAL MESSAGE TO THE READER

W hy did I write this book? When I was in third grade, I was tested in grade school by two ladies for being a genius and/or having ESP. The results showed I am borderline genius and borderline ESP.

When I found out the results, I knew my main purpose in life is to discover the spiritual truth. I knew I wanted to nurture my soul rather than be materialistic. The truth excited me rather than throwing my life away by being materialistic. The materials are temporary; whereas, nurturing my soul is eternal.

I searched out the truth throughout my life because I am hungry for spiritual concepts. I have had fun, thrills, and adventures in my life seeking out spiritual truth. This is an eternal process.

I knew I wanted to share these messages when I had enough spiritual truths to share.

Along the way, friends advised me to write a book. The book idea had never really interested me until I heard a webinar by a gentleman a little over a year ago. He is an inspiration. The book idea fascinated me.

At the beginning of 2018, I knew it would be a great year and that I would fulfill a purpose. This purpose is to share the spiritual messages I have unlocked whether it be through experiences, research, or deep inside myself.

In February of 2018, it struck me. I had a strong urge to write this book and share these messages. I wrote this book based on my lifelong discoveries. This is a lifelong goal for me. I also want to start an online business based off this book, but I want it to be more interactive. I will also be writing more books about spiritual truths in the future.

I hope you enjoyed this book just as much as I enjoy spreading the messages of this spiritual book. I hope I have empowered you to empower yourselves. Since I can make it through the challenges I wrote about in my book, you can too. I wrote about many tools. I hope some, if not all, will assist you through these challenges. I encourage you to do your own research and to see what resonates for you in my book. Filter out what does not work.

Thank you for taking the time to read my book. Stay tuned for future books. If you enjoyed this book, I am sure you will enjoy the books I write in the future. Also, stay tuned for my online business.

God bless you.
Love and light.
*Jennifer Diebold*

# REVIEWS

Now that you have read *The Journey to Enlightenment: Transcending the Dark Nights of the Soul,* may I ask you one favor? Please post a review on Amazon. Just type my full name or title of book on Amazon. Then scroll down to the reviews section.

Please send me your email address to dejavujd17@gmail.com if you loved this book, so I can keep you updated on books I write in the future.

Thank you so kindly.

God bless.
Love and light.
*Jennifer Diebold*

# ABOUT THE AUTHOR

Jennifer Diebold has always known there was more to life than meets the eye. Jennifer Diebold is a student of life as she has always been hungry for spiritual truth. She knows she has a greater purpose in life because she was born awakened. She incarnated on Earth to be part of the wave of souls for ascension and ultimately enlightenment. She enjoys nature, animals, spending time with her soul tribe, meditating, and Kundalini yoga. Jennifer Diebold lives with her cat, Rockstar, who is her best friend other than herself.

# RESORCES

## SECTION 2

1. Summit Publications, 2018, "How To Use the Violet Flame in 9 Easy Steps", www.summitlighthouse.org

## SECTION 3

2. Beckler, Melanie, 2017, "The 11 Types of Lightworkers Helping Earth Ascend", askangels.com You Tube

## SECTION 5

3. Imelda, 2018, "Angel Number 1010 and its Meaning", https://trustedpsychicmediums.com/angel-numbers/angel-number-1010-meaning/

4. Willow Soul heals, 2016, "5 Reasons Why You Are Seeing 11:11 – The Meaning of 1111", willowsoul.com

5. Willow Soul heals, 2017, "3 Reasons Why You Are Seeing 12:12 – The Meaning of 1212", https://willowsoul.com/.../3-reasons-why-you-are-seeing-12-12-the-meaning-of-1212

6. Willow Soul heals, 2017, "3 Reasons Why You Are Seeing 12:34 – The Meaning of 1234", https://willowsoul.com/.../3 reasons-why-you-are-seeing-12-34-the-meaning-of-1234

## SECTION 6

7. Antera- Center for Soul Evolution, 2007, "Twin Flames", Center for Soul Evolution>twin flames, www.soulevolution.org

8. Cornacchia, Michele, 2016, "The Traits and the Qualities of the Divine Masculine", I AM my Soul>blog>the-traits-and-the qualities, http://www.iammysoul.com/

www.ingramcontent.com/pod-product-compliance
Lightning Source LLC
LaVergne TN
LVHW052024080426
835513LV00018B/2150